Collins

Sociology

AQA GCSE Revision

Sociology

AQA GCSE

Revision Guide

Pauline Wilson

About this Revision Guide & Workbook

Revise

These pages provide a recap of everything you need to know for each topic.

You should read through all the information before taking the Quick Test at the end. This will test whether you can recall the key facts.

Practise

These topic-based questions appear shortly after the revision pages for each topic and will test whether you have understood the topic. If you get any of the questions wrong, make sure you read the correct answer carefully.

Review

These topic-based questions appear later in the book, allowing you to revisit the topic and test how well you have remembered the information. If you get any of the questions wrong, make sure you read the correct answer carefully.

Mix it Up

These pages feature a mix of questions from the different topics. They will make sure you can recall the relevant information to answer a question without being told which topic it relates to.

Test Yourself on the Go

Visit our website at www.collins.co.uk/collinsGCSErevision and print off a set of flashcards. These pocket-sized cards feature questions and answers so that you can test yourself on all the key facts anytime and anywhere. You will also find lots more information about the advantages of spaced practice and how to plan for it.

Workbook

This section features even more topic-based questions as well as practice exam papers, providing two further practice opportunities for each topic to guarantee the best results.

ebook

To access the ebook revision guide visit

www.collins.co.uk/ebooks

and follow the step-by-step instructions.

Exam Assessment

The AQA GCSE 9-1 Sociology Exam

The GCSE Sociology exam is made up of two papers.

Paper 1 assesses:	**Paper 2** assesses:
Section A: The sociology of families	**Section A:** The sociology of crime and deviance
Section B: The sociology of education	**Section B:** The sociology of social stratification
Relevant areas of social theory and methods are assessed in both sections.	Relevant areas of social theory and methods are assessed in both sections.
• Written exam: 1 hour and 45 minutes • Marked out of 100 • 50% of the GCSE	• Written exam: 1 hour and 45 minutes • Marked out of 100 • 50% of the GCSE
• Section A and Section B each have two multiple choice questions followed by a range of short and extended responses. • All questions are compulsory.	• Section A and Section B each have two multiple choice questions followed by a range of short and extended responses. • All questions are compulsory.

The Skills You Are Assessed On

When the examiners mark your answers, they are looking for particular skills. These are called assessment objectives (AOs). In both Paper 1 and Paper 2, you will be assessed on your:

Knowledge and Understanding (AO1)
- You must show that you know and understand the subject matter (the theories, key thinkers, methods, key terms, concepts and evidence) that you have been studying.

Application (AO2)
- You must also show that you can apply your knowledge to the set question. This involves using what you know about an issue in order to address the set question.

Analysis and Evaluation (AO3)
You must show that you can:
- make sense of any written and statistical information presented to you
- draw on other relevant topics to show how the different areas of sociology are related to each other
- assess an explanation or an idea by identifying its strengths and weaknesses
- evaluate one approach to a question or issue by comparing and contrasting it to other relevant approaches
- reach a judgement or a balanced conclusion.

Command Words

The command words in an exam question tell you exactly what the examiners will be looking for in your answer and which skills you must demonstrate in order to earn full marks.

Here are some examples of command words along with an explanation of how you should respond to these words.

1. **Identify...** State a point briefly or name
2. **Describe...** Set out the main features or characteristics; give an account of
3. **From Item B...** Draw on relevant material – but do not just copy it out!
4. **Identify and explain one reason why...** Briefly state a relevant reason and develop this by discussing the reason in more depth
5. **Discuss how far sociologists agree...** Explain one side of the debate and criticise it, present other sides of the debate and come to a conclusion.

Contents

Contents

The Sociological Approach

You must be able to:

- Explain what sociology involves
- Explain what social structures, social processes and social issues are
- Explain the terms culture, values, norms and socialisation.

Defining Sociology

- Sociology is often defined as the study of **society**. A society is a group of people who share a **culture** or a way of life.
- Sociology explores the social factors that shape human behaviour, the ways in which society influences people's lives and the ways in which people shape society.
- Sociologists examine society's **social structures** (or the different parts that make up society). Social structures include families, the education system, the criminal justice system and the social stratification system.
  - Sociologists explore the connections or relationships between these parts, such as the relationship between students' family backgrounds and their achievements at GCSE.
- Sociology asks questions about **social processes** such as socialisation, labelling and social control.
- Sociologists explore the **social issues** facing people in their daily lives, such as the quality of parenting, care of the elderly, violent crime and poverty.

Sociology puts society under the magnifying glass.

Making Sense of the Social World

- In trying to make sense of the social world, sociologists use:
  - a body of terms (specialised vocabulary) and concepts (key ideas)
  - a body of theories about the relationship between the individual and society
  - a tool kit of research methods (such as questionnaires, interviews and observation) to gather evidence in an organised and systematic way. As a result, sociology can provide factual information that is more reliable than information from other sources.

Key Point

Psychologists study people and their behaviour, and base their explanations on evidence from research. They focus on individual behaviour and study topics like mental illness. In contrast, sociologists study social influences on human life and focus on group behaviour.

Culture

- The term culture refers to the whole way of life of a particular society. It includes society's **values**, **norms**, customs, beliefs, knowledge, skills and language.
- Culture varies according to place (where you are) and time period (when). For example, roast guinea pig is a traditional delicacy in Ecuador, while guinea pigs are often kept as family pets in the UK.

Values

- Values are ideas and beliefs about what is desirable and worth striving for. Examples include the value placed on top examination grades, privacy and respect for human life. Values provide general guidelines for behaviour.
- Values vary cross-culturally – they differ from one culture to another. In Western societies, for example, wealth and material possessions are often highly valued and considered worth striving for.

Norms

- Norms provide guidelines on appropriate and expected behaviour in specific social settings such as classrooms, cinemas, restaurants and aeroplanes. In a cinema, for example, people are usually expected to sit quietly while watching the film. Norms provide order in society and allow it to function smoothly.
- Norms are enforced by **sanctions** (rewards and punishments).
  - Positive sanctions reward people for conforming to (or following) the norms, for example via promotion at work.
  - Negative sanctions punish people who deviate from (or break) the norms, for example by giving them a verbal warning.

Socialisation

- The term **socialisation** refers to the process by which people learn the culture, values and norms of society.

Type of socialisation	Definition	Agencies (groups or institutions)
Primary socialisation	Early childhood learning, during which babies and infants learn the basic behaviour patterns, language and skills they will need in later life.	**Agencies of primary socialisation** are usually families and parents. Through interaction within their families, children acquire language and other essential skills.
Secondary socialisation	Begins later in childhood and continues throughout adulthood. Through this process, people learn society's norms and values.	**Agencies of secondary socialisation** include peer groups, schools, workplaces, religions and the **mass media**.

> ## Key Point
>
> As you work through the topics in this book, try to look out for connections or links between them. For example, socialisation is linked to families, education and gender.

> ## Key Words
>
> society
> culture
> social structures
> social processes
> social issues
> values
> norms
> sanctions
> socialisation
> primary socialisation
> agencies of primary socialisation
> secondary socialisation
> agencies of secondary socialisation
> mass media

> ## Quick Test
>
> 1. Identify one example of a social process.
> 2. Sanctions provide guidelines on appropriate and expected behaviour in social settings such as cinemas, restaurants or aeroplanes. True or false?
> 3. Which term do sociologists use to describe the process by which people learn their society's culture, norms and values?

The Key Ideas of Marx and Durkheim

You must be able to:

- Describe the key ideas of Karl Marx
- Describe the key ideas of Émile Durkheim
- Outline the criticisms of Marxism and the functionalist approach.

The Key Ideas of Karl Marx

- Karl Marx's ideas inspired the Marxist perspective, or **Marxism**. He wrote at an early stage in the development of **capitalism** and wanted to explain the **social changes** taking place at that time.
- Marx argued that to understand the development of societies, it is necessary to examine how people produce the things they need to subsist. The term 'mode of production' refers to the way people produce the means of their subsistence.
- Marx identified two key aspects of a mode of production: the **means of production** and the social relations of production.
  - The means of production are the materials that people use in production. Under the **capitalist** mode of production, these include capital, big businesses, machinery, factories and land.
  - The social relations of production are the relationships between people as they engage in production. Under capitalism, the two main social classes are the **bourgeoisie** and the **proletariat**.

Social Classes under Capitalism

- The bourgeoisie – the minority capitalist or ruling class – own the means of production and private property.
- The proletariat – the majority working class – own nothing other than their ability to work as wage labourers.
- Other classes include the **petty bourgeoisie**, who own small businesses, and the **lumpenproletariat**, the 'dropouts' who sometimes sell their services to the bourgeoisie.
- The bourgeoisie exploit the proletariat by profiting from their labour. Marx argued that the gap in the resources of the bourgeoisie and the proletariat would widen over time. The petty bourgeoisie would be unable to compete with bigger companies and would sink into the proletariat.
- Marx argued that the **class struggle** between the proletariat and the bourgeoisie was the key to social change. Eventually, members of the proletariat would develop class consciousness, come to see themselves as a social class with common interests and would overthrow the capitalist class. This would lead to a period of social revolution and the move to **communism**.
- Under communism, the means of production would be held communally rather than by a minority. In this situation, there would be a **classless society** with neither private ownership nor exploitation.

 Key Thinker

Karl Marx (1818–1883)

 Key Point

Capitalism is an economic system in which private owners of capital invest money in businesses to make a profit. Marx was critical of capitalism and wanted a fair society.

Criticisms of Marx

- Marx saw social class as based on economic divisions. However, critics such as Weber argue that class is also based on status (social standing or prestige) differences between groups.
- Marx overlooked social divisions based on gender and ethnicity.
- Critics argue that a revolution has not occurred in capitalist societies such as Britain and that Marx's ideas are now outdated.

The Key Ideas of Émile Durkheim

- Durkheim was a main figure in the origins of functionalism.
- Functionalism sees society as made up of different parts that fit together. It examines institutions such as the family, education and religion in terms of their functions, that is, the job they perform to help society run smoothly. These institutions meet the needs of society by performing functions to ensure its survival.
- Functionalism focuses on the positive rather than the negative functions that the different structures perform in society.
- Durkheim studied crime, religion and education by focusing on the functions they fulfil in meeting the needs of society.
  - For example, the punishment of criminals has an important function in helping to bring people together. Punishment reinforces the values and beliefs that the majority of people in society hold. By binding people together in this way, crime can contribute to social cohesion.

Punishing criminals can bind the majority of law-abiding people together.

Criticisms of the Functionalist Approach

- Functionalism overlooks the dysfunctional (or negative) aspects of things like crime and religion. In reality, crime and religion do not always perform positive functions for society.
- Critics argue that functionalist theories are now outdated.

Revise

Key Thinker

Émile Durkheim
(1858–1917)

Key Point

Marx and Durkheim are two of the founders of sociology. They wrote during times of rapid social and economic change (such as the development of capitalism and industrialisation from around the middle of the eighteenth century) and their work attempts to make sense of these changes. It is important that you are familiar with their key ideas and perspectives.

Key Words

Marxism
capitalism
social changes
means of production
capitalist
bourgeoisie
proletariat
petty bourgeoisie
lumpenproletariat
class struggle
communism
classless society
functionalism
social cohesion

Quick Test

1. Identify one difference between the bourgeoisie and the proletariat.
2. Identify one function of punishment, according to Durkheim.

Other Sociological Approaches

You must be able to:

- Describe the key ideas of Max Weber
- Discuss feminist perspectives in sociology
- Outline the consensus versus conflict debate.

The Key Ideas of Max Weber

- Weber made a major contribution to several sociological topics including social class, status and power.
- Like Marx, Weber was interested in issues such as the development of capitalism and social class.

Social Class, Status and Power

- Both Marx and Weber defined class in terms of economic factors.
  - Weber agreed with Marx that ownership and non-ownership of property is the most important basis of class divisions.
  - However, Weber argued that class divisions are not based solely on economic factors. They are also linked to skills and qualifications, which affect the jobs that people get. People with high-level qualifications (such as university degrees) and specialised skills (such as surgeons or architects) are in a stronger position in the labour market than those without.
- Weber saw status as another aspect of social stratification in addition to class. Status refers to how much prestige or social standing a group has. Groups such as judges have high status in society.
  - Weber argued that status does not always go hand-in-hand with income. Some groups (such as second-hand car dealers) earn high incomes but have relatively low status in society. Others, such as religious leaders, have high status but low incomes.
- Weber argued that an individual or group exercises power when they can get what they want, despite any opposition from others. People have power in so far as they can get other people to behave as they want them to.

Criticism of Weber

- Weber focused on class divisions in society. He did not explore inequalities based on gender, ethnicity or age in detail.

Theoretical Perspectives in Sociology

Sociologists disagree about how they see the social world, so there are different theoretical perspectives in sociology. A perspective is a particular way of seeing society and explaining how it works. Examples include functionalism, Marxism and feminism.

Key Thinker

Max Weber (1864–1920)

Weber argued that class divisions are based on skills and qualifications as well as ownership or non-ownership of private property.

Key Point

Max Weber is one of the founders of sociology. Like Marx and Durkheim, he wrote during times of rapid social and economic change, and his work attempts to make sense of these changes. It is important that you are familiar with his key ideas.

Feminist Perspectives

- Feminist sociologists explore gender inequality, sexism and discrimination in society.
- They see sex and gender as different categories.
  - The term 'sex' refers to biological differences between males and females (for example, their roles in reproduction).
  - Gender refers to the different cultural expectations, ideas and practices linked to masculinity and femininity.
- Some feminist approaches see society as patriarchal. In a patriarchal society, men have power over, and dominate, women.

The Consensus Versus Conflict Debate

- One key difference between the theoretical perspectives is whether they see society as based on consensus (agreement and harmony) or conflict (disagreement and lack of harmony). The consensus approach sees society in positive terms but the conflict approach is critical of the way society is organised.
- According to the consensus approach, order and stability in society depend on cooperation between individuals and groups who work together for the common good.
  - Functionalism sees society as based on value consensus. In other words, people agree with society's norms and values. This consensus arises from the socialisation process during which people learn society's norms and values.
  - Functionalism argues that social order is based on consensus. Order is maintained over time because most people support the rules and agree to stick (conform) to them.
- Marxism and feminism are examples of conflict theories that see society as based on conflicting interests between groups rather than on consensus.
  - The Marxist perspective sees capitalist societies as based on class conflict between the bourgeoisie and the proletariat. However, social order is maintained over time partly because the bourgeoisie have the power to enforce order. They are able, for instance, to influence the type of laws that are passed.
  - Some feminist approaches argue that society is patriarchal. In other words, it is based on male power over women. These approaches explore the workings of patriarchy within social structures such as families, education, the workplace and the criminal justice system. They see family life, for example, as based on male dominance which is reflected in men's control of decision-making and in domestic violence.

Key Words
social class
status
power
social stratification
theoretical perspectives
feminism
feminist
gender
sexism
discrimination
consensus
value consensus
patriarchy

Quick Test

1. Identify one similarity between Marx's and Weber's views on social class.
2. Identify one difference between functionalist and Marxist perspectives.
3. Identify one similarity between Marxist and feminist perspectives.

Research Design

You must be able to:

- Describe and explain the different stages of the research process
- Show an understanding of ethical issues.

The Importance of the Research Process

- Sociologists carry out **research** in order to collect **data** systematically.
- This data provides evidence to help them explain the social world.

The Stages of the Research Process

Stage	Details
Developing research aims or hypotheses	- Research aims set out what the researcher intends to investigate and provide the study's focus. - A **hypothesis** is a hunch or an informed guess. It is written as a testable statement that will either be supported by the evidence or proved wrong.

Choosing a research method or methods	- Choice of methods is influenced by practical issues such as time and money, ethical issues and theoretical issues. One key theoretical issue relates to the debates about **positivism** and **interpretivism**.
	  – Positivists favour a scientific approach when studying the social world. By generating hypotheses and testing them, sociologists can discover the facts. Positivists prefer quantitative methods such as social surveys which are designed to gather facts and to describe society in statistical terms.
	  – Interpretivists aim to understand human behaviour by exploring what it means to those involved. They prefer qualitative methods such as in-depth interviews and participant observation that collect rich, detailed accounts.

Carrying out a pilot study	- A pilot study is a small-scale trial run carried out before the main research. It allows the researcher to test the chosen methods and ensure that they are appropriate and cost-effective.

Selecting a sample	- Rather than study the whole **population**, a researcher often selects a **sample** by using a sampling technique.
	  – Random sampling: each member of the sampling frame has a known chance of being selected. A **random sample** is likely to be representative of the population and generalisations can be drawn from it. Examples include simple random sampling (each member of the population has the same chance of being included in the sample) and **systematic sampling** (taking every 'nth' item from the sampling frame).
	  – Non-probability sampling: used when a sampling frame is unavailable. The sample is not selected randomly so it is unlikely to mirror the population. Examples include a **snowball sample** (contacting one member of the population and identifying others through them) and a **quota sample** (including a quota of women or teenagers, for example, in proportion to their numbers in the population).

	– A **representative sample** is typical of its wider population. If the **sampling frame** is inaccurate (for example, incomplete or out of date), it may generate an **unrepresentative sample**. This would make it difficult to generalise from the sample to the population.
Collecting the data	• This involves gathering raw data to use as evidence. Sociologists collect **primary data** by using research methods such as questionnaires or observation. • They may also draw on **secondary data** or pre-existing sources collected by other people (such as official statistics). • Sociologists may use **quantitative data** and/or **qualitative data** from the various primary and secondary sources. **Mixed methods research** generates both quantitative and qualitative data within one study. **Triangulation** involves cross-checking the findings from a qualitative method against the findings from a quantitative method.
Analysing the data	• **Data analysis** involves interpreting or making sense of the information and summarising the main findings or results.
Evaluating the research	• Sociological research outputs (for example, journal articles and conference papers) are reviewed and evaluated by other sociologists. This peer review is a form of quality control.

Research Ethics

- **Ethical considerations** relate to morals and are important in the research process. Sociologists are expected to respect and safeguard participants' interests.
- Important principles include **informed consent**, anonymity, privacy and **confidentiality**.
- Principles of **data protection** apply to all information collected during the research process.

For some groups (such as homeless people), a sampling frame is not available and the sample cannot be selected randomly.

Quick Test

1. With a simple random sample, each member of the population has an equal chance of being selected. True or false?
2. With snowball sampling, researchers take every 'nth' item from the sampling frame, for example every 20th name from a school register. True or false?
3. With systematic sampling, the researcher contacts one member of a population (for example, one member of a criminal subculture) and later identifies others in the same population. True or false?

Key Words

research	unrepresentative sample
data	
hypothesis	primary data
positivism	secondary data
interpretivism	quantitative data
population	qualitative data
sample	mixed methods research
random sample	triangulation
systematic sampling	data analysis
snowball sample	ethical considerations
quota sample	informed consent
representative sample	confidentiality
sampling frame	data protection

Quantitative Methods

You must be able to:

- Describe what a social survey, questionnaire, structured interview and longitudinal study involve
- Explain their uses, advantages and disadvantages.

Social Surveys

- A **social survey** consists of a list of standardised questions. Each **respondent** answers an identical set of questions.
- Surveys are usually used to collect quantitative data.
- There are two main ways of carrying out surveys:
  1. self-completion **questionnaires** delivered by post, via email or by hand
  2. structured or formal **interviews** delivered face-to-face or by telephone.

Different Types of Survey Question

- **Closed questions** require the respondent to choose between several given answers, possibly by ticking a box. The responses are relatively easy to process by computer and summarise in statistical form. The questions and answers must be worded clearly and all possible answers must be included.
- **Open-ended questions** allow respondents to give their own (longer and more detailed) answers to the set questions. Responses are likely to be varied and more difficult to convert into statistics.

Advantages and Disadvantages of Questionnaires and Structured Interviews

Advantages	Disadvantages
• With standardised questions, respondents' answers can be compared to identify differences in attitudes or opinions. • Closed questions provide quantitative data and the answers can be presented in numerical form, for example in graphs. It is possible to measure the strength of a connection between different factors, for example between support for the government and **trade union** membership. • Replication: the questions are standardised, so a survey can be repeated to check for **reliability**. If the results are consistent a second time round, they are seen as reliable. • With reliable results, sociologists can generalise from the sample to the population.	• Surveys use pre-set questions which do not allow any new issues to emerge. • With closed questions, the researcher decides not only the questions but also the possible answers in advance. • Closed questions do not let respondents explain why they ticked a particular box. • The results may lack validity because, for example, what people say about their behaviour may not reflect how they behave in their everyday lives. • Some feminist researchers such as Ann Oakley see structured interviews as based on unequal power relationships between the interviewer (who asks the questions) and the respondents (who are expected to answer rather than ask questions).

Key Point

Quantitative methods such as questionnaires and structured interviews collect data in numerical form. The results are usually displayed in graphs, pie charts, bar charts or tables of statistics that count or measure something. Qualitative methods such as unstructured interviews and participant observation collect rich, detailed data in the form of words or quotations.

Advantages and Disadvantages of Postal Questionnaires

Advantages	Disadvantages
• A quick and cheap way of getting information from large samples spread over a wide area. • The researcher is not present so respondents may not feel under pressure to give socially acceptable answers.	• The respondent may misunderstand or skip questions. • The questionnaire might not be completed by the person it was sent to. • Unsuitable for some populations (e.g. illiterate or homeless people). • The response rate (the number of replies received in proportion to the total number of questionnaires distributed) is usually low. Those who respond may not be representative or typical of the population being studied. If so, the researcher cannot make generalisations.

Advantages and Disadvantages of Structured Interviews Compared to Postal Questionnaires

Advantages	Disadvantages
• Interviewers can explain what the questions mean. • They can ensure that all relevant questions are completed. • Structured interviews do not exclude people with literacy problems.	• Interview bias: the interview situation itself may influence the respondents to give socially acceptable answers (known as social desirability). Respondents might not reveal their true thoughts or behaviour. • Interviewer bias: the interviewer's age, gender, ethnicity or accent may influence the respondent's answers. In cases of interview and interviewer bias, the results will lack validity – they will not provide a true or authentic picture of the topic under study.

Longitudinal Studies

- A **longitudinal study** follows the same group of people over time. After the initial survey or interview has taken place, follow-up surveys or interviews are carried out at intervals over several years.
- They allow researchers to study changes in individuals' behaviour, values and opinions over time.

Disadvantages of Longitudinal Studies
- Longitudinal studies are relatively expensive and time-consuming.
- There are problems in maintaining contact with the original sample over time.
- People may change their minds and decide to withdraw from the study.

Quick Test

1. Identify one advantage of using closed questions in a survey.
2. State one disadvantage of a longitudinal study.
3. Identify one similarity between a structured interview and a postal questionnaire.

> **Revise**

Think about why positivist sociologists might use social surveys.

> ### Key Point
>
> Interviews may be structured, semi-structured or unstructured depending on how far the questions are standardised in advance. Structured interviews provide quantitative data and unstructured interviews provide qualitative data.

Surveys are a popular research method.

> ### Key Words
>
> social survey
> respondent
> questionnaires
> interviews
> closed questions
> open-ended questions
> trade union
> reliability
> bias
> validity
> longitudinal study

Qualitative Methods

You must be able to:

- Explain the uses, advantages and disadvantages of unstructured and group interviews
- Explain the uses, advantages and disadvantages of participant and non-participant observation.

Interviews in Qualitative Research

- In qualitative research, sociologists use in-depth interviews which range from completely unstructured to loosely or semi-structured.

Advantages and Disadvantages of Unstructured Interviews

Advantages	Disadvantages
• Interviewers can probe, ask follow-up questions and explore complex issues. • Interviewees can develop their answers and introduce issues that the researcher had not thought of. • By exploring how interviewees understand their own experiences, sociologists can obtain rich, detailed and valid data. • Sociologists can build a stronger rapport with the interviewees, allowing them to investigate sensitive topics.	• Relatively time-consuming and expensive for the amount of data collected. • They need a skilled interviewer to keep the conversation going and encourage interviewees to open up. • If interview or interviewer bias occurs, the results will be invalid. • The sample is usually small and unrepresentative. • Without a standardised schedule, it is virtually impossible to replicate an unstructured interview in order to check the reliability of the findings. Consequently, it is difficult to make generalisations.

<table>
<tr><td>

Key Point

In a group interview, the researcher questions several people about various topics. A **focus group** concentrates on one particular topic. It explores how people interact within the group and respond to each other's views.

</td><td>

A focus group concentrates on one topic and explores how participants respond to each other's views.

</td><td>

Key Point

Unstructured interviews are popular among some feminist sociologists. Ann Oakley (1974) prefers in-depth rather than structured interviews because the relationship between the interviewer and interviewee is more equal.

</td></tr>
</table>

Advantages and Disadvantages of Group Interviews

Advantages	Disadvantages
• Researchers can access a wide range of views and experiences. • Interviewing people together saves time and money. • Individuals may feel more comfortable discussing their experiences in a group setting.	• The researcher must manage group interviews carefully, particularly when the topics are sensitive. • The interviewees may influence each other and some may dominate discussions. • The researcher cannot guarantee confidentiality.

Participant Observation

- In a **participant observation** (PO) study, the researcher joins a group and participates in its daily activities in order to investigate it.
  - With overt PO, the group is aware of the researcher's identity.
  - With **covert observation**, group members are not informed that they are taking part in a study. This may be the only way to study criminal groups. Critics, however, argue that it is unethical because it invades people's privacy and is not based on informed consent.

> Think about why interpretivist sociologists might use unstructured interviews or participant observation.

Advantages and Disadvantages of Participant Observation

Advantages	Disadvantages
<ul><li>The researcher can study a group in its natural everyday settings and observe its activities as they occur. The term **ethnography** refers to the study of people's culture and practices in everyday settings.</li><li>A PO study is usually carried out over time. Researchers build up trust and see and hear things that they would not normally have access to.</li><li>By participating in the group's activities, the researcher can see things from group members' perspectives and develop a deeper understanding of their behaviour.</li><li>By giving a true picture of the meanings behind behaviour, PO gathers valid data.</li></ul>	<ul><li>It may be difficult to gain entry to the group and to develop trust.</li><li>PO is a relatively time-consuming and expensive method.</li><li>The observer effect – with overt PO, the researcher's presence may influence the group's behaviour. In this case, the validity of the findings will be affected.</li><li>The researcher may become so involved with the group that the findings are biased or one-sided. In this case, over-involvement would invalidate the findings.</li><li>A PO study is unique and it would be impossible to replicate it to check the reliability of the findings. So it is difficult to generalise about similar groups.</li></ul>

Non-participant Observation

- With **non-participant observation**, the researcher studies the group by observing its activities in a natural setting without participating in them.

Advantages and Disadvantages of Non-participant Observation

Advantages	Disadvantages
<ul><li>Non-participant observers directly observe people's behaviour in natural settings such as classrooms rather than relying on what interviewees tell them.</li><li>They can take notes freely.</li><li>They are less likely than participant observers to get too drawn into the group's activities.</li><li>Non-participant observers may be more objective (less influenced by their personal feelings about the group) than participant observers.</li></ul>	<ul><li>Non-participant observers are less likely than participant observers to understand things in the same way as group members.</li><li>The observer effect may invalidate the findings.</li></ul>

Key Words

focus group
unstructured interviews
participant observation
covert observation
ethnography
non-participant
  observation

Quick Test

1. What do sociologists mean by interview bias?
2. Describe what sociologists mean by the observer effect.

Secondary Sources of Data

You must be able to:

- Explain the uses, advantages and disadvantages of official statistics
- Discuss the uses, advantages and disadvantages of other secondary data
- Explain the uses, advantages and disadvantages of content analysis.

Official Statistics

- Official statistics such as crime and birth rates are an example of quantitative secondary data.
- They are compiled by government departments and agencies such as the Office for National Statistics (ONS).

Advantages and Disadvantages of Official Statistics

Key Point

Non-official statistics are a source of quantitative secondary data produced by non-governmental bodies, e.g. banks and charities.

Advantages	Disadvantages
<ul><li>Save time and money because they already exist and are readily available.</li><li>Based on large samples and are therefore more likely to be representative. The **census**, for example, provides statistical information about the full population.</li><li>Allow sociologists to investigate **trends** over time in areas such as divorce, **unemployment** and **underemployment**.</li><li>Can be combined with qualitative data in mixed methods research.</li></ul>	<ul><li>Might not tell sociologists exactly what they want to know about a particular issue. Divorce statistics, for example, provide information about the number of divorces recorded each year but exclude **empty shell marriages**.</li><li>Interpretivist sociologists argue that official statistics on divorce or unemployment tell us nothing about what it means to the individuals involved to be divorced or unemployed.</li><li>Sociologists cannot check the validity of official statistics. Some statistics (such as birth rates) are likely to give a valid or true picture. Statistics on domestic violence, however, may not give an accurate measurement of its extent.</li><li>Interpretivist sociologists argue that official statistics are a **social construct**. In other words, the statistics are the outcome of decisions made by the various people involved in their construction. Crime statistics, for example, are the outcome of decisions made by people such as victims and police officers.</li></ul>

Quantitative Data Collected by Other Researchers

- Rather than collecting primary data themselves, sociologists can analyse data that other researchers have collected.
- Quantitative data from large, high-quality surveys can be accessed online.

Advantages and Disadvantages of Quantitative Data Collected by Other Researchers

Advantages	Disadvantages
<ul><li>Researchers can save time and money by analysing pre-existing data from surveys rather than collecting data from scratch.</li><li>Many of the data sets (such as the Millennium Cohort Study) are of a high quality. They are based on large samples that are reasonably representative.</li><li>It is possible to carry out longitudinal analysis of this data.</li></ul>	<ul><li>The researcher did not collect the data and has no control over its quality or its validity.</li><li>The data was collected for other purposes so some key variables may be missing.</li></ul>

Qualitative Secondary Data

Sources of qualitative secondary data include:

- data from existing research studies
- mass media products such as newspapers and television
- personal documents such as diaries and letters
- material produced via the internet such as email and blogs
- autobiographies and biographies.

Key Point

Sociologists can analyse both quantitative and qualitative data that other researchers have collected.

Advantages and Disadvantages of Qualitative Secondary Data

Advantages	Disadvantages
• Written documents may provide useful background information about the organisations, experiences or events they refer to.	• Written documents such as diaries or autobiographies may be forgeries. If they are genuine, the contents may not be true. • The events described may have been misinterpreted, for example due to the writer's prejudices.

Media products such as newspapers are a source of qualitative secondary data.

Content Analysis

- **Content analysis** is a way of dealing systematically with qualitative secondary sources such as newspapers and advertisements on television.
- Feminist studies of the representation of gender in television advertisements might use content analysis.
  - In this case, the researcher constructs a set of categories in advance, for example 'gives orders/takes orders'.
  - The researcher then works through the advertisements, coding all sections that show a character giving or taking orders.
  - Once the contents have been coded, the researcher counts up the number of times female and male characters do these things.

Advantages and Disadvantages of Content Analysis

Advantages	Disadvantages
• It generates quantitative data and the contents of different products (such as different TV advertisements) can be compared statistically. • The researcher works with a set of categories so the analysis can be replicated to check reliability.	• It can be time-consuming and laborious. • It involves subjective judgements which may create invalid data.

Key Words

census
empty shell marriages
trends
unemployment
underemployment
social construct
content analysis

Quick Test

1. Content analysis generates qualitative data from quantitative sources. True or false?
2. Crime rates are more likely than birth rates to be valid. True or false?

The Sociological Approach

1 Identify and describe **one** example of a norm. [3]

_____

_____

_____

_____

_____

_____

The Key Ideas of Marx and Durkheim

2 Describe what sociologists mean by social cohesion. [3]

_____

_____

_____

_____

_____

_____

Other Sociological Approaches

3 Describe **one** example of patriarchy within families. [3]

_____

_____

_____

_____

_____

_____

_____

Research Design

4 Describe informed consent within the research process. [3]

_____

_____

_____

_____

_____

_____

_____

_____

Quantitative Methods

5 Identify and explain **one** advantage of using surveys to investigate people's experiences as victims of crime. [4]

Qualitative Methods

6 Identify and explain **one** advantage of using observation to investigate the interaction between teachers and students in classrooms. [4]

Secondary Sources of Data

7 Identify and explain **one** disadvantage of using content analysis to investigate the representation of gender in magazines. [4]

Different Family Forms

You must be able to:

- Explain the term 'family'
- Describe the different types of family in the UK
- Explain the work of Rapoport and Rapoport on family diversity
- Identify alternatives to the family.

Defining a Family and a Household

- The term **family** can be defined as a couple who are married, civil partners or cohabiting, with or without dependent children, or a lone parent with their child or children.
- A household contains either one person living alone or a group of people (for instance, a family or students) who live together.
- Alternatives to families include children's homes and residential care homes, as well as one-person households.

> **Key Point**
>
> Some sociologists use the term 'families' rather than 'the family' to highlight the diversity or variety of family forms in the UK today.

Different Family Types in the UK Today

Nuclear family	A two-generational family containing a heterosexual married or cohabiting couple and their child or children who live together.
Extended family	A group of relatives extending beyond the nuclear family.
	Classic extended family: three generations live together or nearby.
	Modified extended family: members live apart geographically but have regular contact and support.
Reconstituted family	A blended or step family in which one or both partners have a child or children from a previous relationship living with them.
Lone-parent family	A family in which one parent lives with their child or children.
Same-sex family	A family in which a gay or lesbian couple (married, civil partners or cohabiting) live together with their child or children.

An extended family.

Rapoport and Rapoport: Types of Diversity in Families in Britain

Based on their review of the existing literature, Rapoport and Rapoport (1982) identified five types of diversity in families in Britain.

1. Organisational diversity: families vary in their structures, the ways they organise their **domestic division of labour** and their **social networks** such as their links to their extended family. Family structures that illustrate this sort of diversity include conventional nuclear families, one-parent, reconstituted and dual-worker families.

> **Key Thinkers**
>
> Rapoport and Rapoport (1982)

2. **Cultural diversity**: families differ in their cultural values and beliefs. Different minority **ethnic groups** such as those of South Asian and Caribbean heritage illustrate diversity in beliefs and values. These different beliefs and values can affect people's **lifestyles** and ideas about **gender roles**, **child-rearing**, education and paid work.

3. **Social class diversity**: a family's social class position affects the resources available to its members, role relationships between partners, and childrearing practices such as how parents discipline their children.

4. **Life-course diversity**: the stage in the family life-cycle that a particular family has reached. Newlyweds without children, families with young children and retired couples in **empty nest families** are all at different stages in the life-cycle and have different lifestyles.

5. **Cohort diversity**: the particular period of time in which a family passes through different stages of the family life-cycle. For example, over time divorce has lost its **social stigma**, so younger couples may find it easier to get divorced today.

Key Point

The Rapoports are key thinkers, so it is important that you are familiar with their work on **family diversity**, including their research methods. In this study, they drew on secondary sources in the form of research carried out by other sociologists.

Life-course diversity – families at different stages in the family life-cycle.

Global Diversity in Families and Households

- **Cross-cultural studies** show that different family types exist in different cultures.
- In broad terms, a **commune** is a group of people who share living accommodation, possessions, wealth and property.
- A **kibbutz** consists of a group of people who live together communally, and value equality and cooperation between members.

Key Words

family
nuclear family
extended family
reconstituted family
lone-parent family
same-sex family
domestic division of
  labour
social network
cultural diversity
ethnic groups
lifestyles
gender roles
child-rearing
empty nest families
social stigma
family diversity
cross-cultural studies
commune
kibbutz

Quick Test

1. Which research method did Rapoport and Rapoport use in their study of families?
2. What did they focus on in their study of families?
3. Conventional nuclear families and dual-worker families are examples of families that illustrate organisational diversity. True or false?

The Functions of Families

You must be able to:

- Explain the functions of families
- Explain Parsons' functionalist perspective on the nuclear family
- Explain the criticisms of the functionalist view.

The Functionalist Approach to the Functions of Families

- There are different sociological approaches to the study of families. The functionalist approach focuses on the positive functions that the nuclear family performs for individuals and for society. Murdock (1949) identified four essential functions.

  1. **The sexual function:** society needs to regulate sexual activity. The nuclear family regulates a married couple's sexual behaviour and helps to maintain their relationship.

  2. **The reproductive function:** society needs new members if it is to survive over time. The nuclear family produces the next generation of society's members.

  3. **The economic function:** society needs a way of providing people with financial support (for instance, food and shelter). Economic cooperation is based on a division of labour between the husband and wife within a nuclear family.

  4. **The educational function:** society needs to ensure that new members learn its culture. This learning takes place through socialisation within the nuclear family.

The functionalist approach saw the traditional nuclear family (made up of a married couple and their biological children) as a key part of society during the 1940s and 1950s. Today, however, many nuclear families are made up of cohabiting couples and their children.

Parsons' Functionalist Account of the Nuclear Family

- Parsons (1956) identified two basic and vital functions that all families perform in all societies: primary socialisation and the stabilisation of adult personalities.

  1. The nuclear family functions as an agency of primary socialisation. Through this process, children learn the culture of their society. The family is vital because it socialises children so that they learn and accept society's shared values and roles. This helps to maintain the stability of society.

  2. The nuclear family functions as an agency of personality stabilisation (the stabilisation of adult personalities). Everyday life outside the family can be stressful for adults and can put them under pressure. However, the husband and wife support each other emotionally and this relieves the pressure. (This is also known as the 'warm bath' theory.) In this way, the family is a safe haven and plays a key role in maintaining the emotional stability of adults. Also, by living with children, parents can act out the childish elements of their own personality. This also helps to keep adult personalities stable.

Key Thinker
Parsons (1956)

Emotional support from a spouse may help to relieve the pressures of everyday life.

Criticisms of Parsons, Murdock and the Functionalist Perspective

- Critics see functionalist accounts as outdated, unrealistic and sexist.
- Parsons focuses on American middle-class families and ignores social class, and religious and ethnic diversity.
- Parsons ignores alternatives to the nuclear family (such as communes or kibbutzim) that could fulfil the two functions.
- Idealisation – Parsons gives an idealised view of families that does not match the reality. He ignores dysfunctional families in which there is conflict, emotional stress, child abuse and domestic violence.
- Marxists are critical of the nuclear family and see it as functional for capitalist society. In their view, one of its functions is to socialise children into accepting the values of capitalism. In this way, the nuclear family serves the interests of capitalism.
- Many feminists see the family as a major source of female oppression. Nuclear families imprison women in their own homes, where they are tied to childcare and housework.

How relevant do you think Parsons' ideas are today?

Key Point

Parsons is a key thinker, so it is important that you are familiar with his work on the functions of the family and the criticisms of his ideas.

Key Words

roles
ethnic diversity
kibbutzim
idealisation
dysfunctional families

Quick Test

1. Identify Parsons' theoretical perspective on the family.
2. In which decade did Parsons' work get published?
3. Parsons identified four basic and vital functions performed by all families in all societies. True or false?

The Marxist Perspective on Families

You must be able to:

- Explain the Marxist approach to families
- Describe the key ideas of Zaretsky
- Explain the criticisms of the Marxist view.

The Marxist Approach to Families

- The Marxist perspective is critical of the nuclear family and its role in maintaining the capitalist system.
- The nuclear family recreates inequalities between social classes over time. For example, members of the bourgeoisie (the owners of the means of production such as land and factories) can buy their children a privileged education and pass on their wealth to the next generation.
- Through socialisation within the family, working-class children learn to accept their lower position in an unequal society and to see the system as fair.

Key Point

The Marxist perspective on families is different from the functionalist perspective in important respects.

Members of the bourgeoisie can buy their children a privileged education. In this way, the family recreates social class inequalities over time.

Zaretsky's Account of the Family

- Zaretsky (1976) writes about the family from a Marxist perspective.
- He argues that, before the early 19th century, the family was a unit of production. For instance, during the early stages of the textile industry, all family members were involved in the production of cloth within the home.
- The rise of industrial capitalism and factory-based production led to a split between family life and work. So the family and the economy are now seen as two separate spheres: the private and the public sphere.

Key Thinker

Zaretsky (1976)

- With the separation of home and work, women became responsible for personal relationships and for family members' emotional well-being.
- The nuclear family has an **economic function** that serves the interests of capitalism. Women undertake unpaid labour within the home (such as child-rearing and cleaning) and maintain daily life. The system of wage labour relies on this unpaid domestic labour. Yet domestic labour is devalued because it is seen as separate from the world of work.
- Through the family, each social class reproduces itself over time. The bourgeois family transmits its private property from one generation to the next (through inheritance). The proletarian family reproduces the labour force by producing future generations of workers.
- The family is a vital unit of consumption for capitalism. Families buy and consume the products of capitalism and enable the bourgeoisie to make profits.
- Zaretsky believes that only **socialism** can end the artificial separation of family life and public life, and make personal fulfilment possible.

Criticisms of the Marxist Approach to Families and Zaretsky

- Marxists ignore the fact that many people are satisfied with family life and **marriage**.
- Feminists argue that Marxists work with the traditional model of the nuclear family – that of the male breadwinner and female housewife. Marxists ignore family diversity.
- Some feminists see female oppression as linked to patriarchy rather than to capitalism.
- Marxists tend to focus on negative aspects of the nuclear family but functionalists see it as meeting the needs of individuals and society. Parsons, for example, saw the nuclear family as a safe haven that provides spouses with emotional support.

> **Key Point**
>
> Zaretsky (1976) is a key thinker, so it is important that you are familiar with his work on the role of the family under capitalism and the criticisms of his ideas.

Critics argue that Marxists overlook people's satisfaction with marriage and family life.

> **Quick Test**
>
> 1. Identify one function of families, according to the Marxist perspective.
> 2. In Zaretsky's view, why is domestic labour devalued?
> 3. Identify one difference between the Marxist and functionalist perspectives on the family.

> **Key Words**
>
> economic function
> socialism
> marriage

Feminist and other Critical Views of Families

You must be able to:

- Explain feminist approaches to the study of families
- Describe the ideas of Delphy and Leonard
- Explain the criticisms of feminist views
- Outline different criticisms of families.

Feminist Approaches to Families

- Feminist perspectives focus on gender relations. They are generally critical of the role of the family in society and its negative impact on women.
- Families actively contribute to the construction of gender differences through primary socialisation processes, for example by dressing girls in pink and boys in blue.
- The term **canalisation** describes the way parents channel their children's interests into toys, games and other activities that are seen as gender appropriate. Through gender socialisation, the family helps to reproduce gender inequalities over time.

Gender socialisation in action.

Key Thinkers

Delphy and Leonard (1992)

Delphy and Leonard's Account of Families and Marriage

- Delphy and Leonard (1992) are radical feminists who argue that the family is patriarchal.
- Family relationships involve economic exploitation. In other words, men benefit from the unpaid work of women within families.
  - Wives are exploited in terms of the way their labour is used by their husbands; their work not being valued; and their financial dependence on their husbands.
- The family is based on a hierarchy – with the husband at the top and other family members in subordinate positions. The husband provides for his wife's upkeep and gets to control her labour for his own use. Even when women have well-paid, full-time employment, they still do most of the domestic work and childcare.
- Families maintain men's dominance over women and children. In this way, the **patriarchal family** maintains the patriarchal nature of society.

Key Point

Delphy and Leonard (1992) drew on existing research in their article on exploitation within families and marriage.

The term **matriarchal family** refers to a family in which power is held by a female (who may be referred to as a **matriarch**).

Criticisms of Feminist Approaches

- Delphy and Leonard do not consider **egalitarian** families that share power between their members.
- Marxist approaches link inequalities within families to capitalism rather than to patriarchy.
- Functionalists see the family as meeting the needs of individuals and society.

Criticisms of Families

- Many sociologists are critical of families.
- Feminists are critical of:
  - the patriarchal nature of families
  - the status and role of women in families
  - the family's role as an agency of gender socialisation.
- Marxists are critical of:
  - the economic function of the nuclear family under capitalism
  - the family's role in reproducing **social inequality** over time
  - the family's role as a unit of consumption for capitalism.

Other Criticisms of Families

- Other sociologists and commentators are critical of or concerned by one or more of the following.
  - The decline in traditional family values, such as the idea that a normal family type is made up of a married couple bringing up their biological children.
  - Social changes such as the increase in marital breakdown, **divorce** and single-parent families. These changes undermine the functions of the family. If the family cannot fulfil its functions (for example, socialisation), this threatens the stability of society as a whole.
  - The **isolation** (or separation) of the nuclear family from the wider **kinship** networks and its loss of contact with the wider family.
  - The loss of traditional functions (such as education and economic production) that families once carried out but which have now been transferred to other structures of society, such as the education system.
  - The functionalist perspective's unrealistic idealisation of the nuclear family. This ignores dysfunctional families in which domestic violence and abuse are found.

Key Point

The feminist perspective on families is similar to the Marxist perspective in some respects and different in others.

Key Words

canalisation
patriarchal family
matriarchal family
matriarch
egalitarian
social inequality
divorce
isolation
kinship

Quick Test

1. Which research method did Delphy and Leonard use in their study of families?
2. What did they focus on in their study of families?
3. Identify one similarity between the Marxist and feminist perspectives on the family.

Conjugal Role Relationships

You must be able to:

- Explain the difference between joint and segregated conjugal roles
- Outline Young and Willmott's views on the symmetrical family
- Outline Oakley's views on conventional families
- Describe how power is distributed in conjugal relationships.

Joint and Segregated Conjugal Roles

- There are two types of conjugal roles: segregated conjugal roles and joint conjugal roles.

Segregated conjugal roles and relationships	Joint conjugal roles and relationships
- A clear division of domestic labour – tasks are divided by gender. - The couple spend little of their leisure time together and have separate interests.	- No rigid division of household tasks into male and female jobs. - The couple share much of their leisure time and have few separate interests.

- During the early 20th century, conjugal roles were segregated. Generally, married women were responsible for domestic labour and men were the main **wage** earners.
- Parsons (1956) argued that the man takes the more **instrumental role** as breadwinner. The woman takes the more **expressive role** as housewife and mother. He explains this in terms of biological differences between the sexes.

Parsons argued that men take the instrumental role as family breadwinners. Remember that he adopts a functionalist perspective.

Young and Willmott's Account of the Symmetrical Family

- Some sociologists suggest that conjugal roles are becoming more joint (**integrated conjugal roles**).
- Young and Willmott (1973) argue that the **symmetrical family** is typical in Britain. Symmetrical relationships are opposite but similar. The spouses perform different tasks but each makes a similar contribution to the home.
  - Decision-making, including financial decisions, is more shared.
  - Family members are now more home-centred, sharing much of their leisure time.

Reasons for the Move to Symmetry

- The rise of feminism since the 1960s influenced women's attitudes and led them to reject the housewife role.
- Legal changes such as the Equal Pay Act (1970) and the Sex Discrimination Act (1975) gave women more equality and status within the workplace.
- More effective birth control enables women to combine motherhood with paid work.
- Technological developments create opportunities for sharing home-based leisure activities such as computer games, so men now spend more time at home.

> ### Key Thinkers
> Young and Willmott (1973)

Young and Willmott's ideas are influenced by the functionalist perspective.

> ### Key Point
> In their research, Young and Willmott (1973) used a questionnaire survey delivered as a face-to-face, structured interview.

Criticisms of Young and Willmott's Account

- Feminists reject the idea of symmetry. For example, Oakley found that women in paid work still had the main responsibility for housework.
- Although attitudes to gender roles may have changed, people's behaviour has not altered much. Many women now work a **double shift**, combining paid work with housework. In practice, the **new man** is hard to find.

Oakley's Views on the Conventional Family

- Oakley (1982) defines the **conventional family** as a nuclear family comprising a married couple and their children who live together.
  - Women are expected to do unpaid work inside the home while men are expected to do paid work outside the home.
  - The man's economic power is linked to his income from paid work.
  - The woman's dependence on the man's wages is one aspect of inequality.
- Statistically, the conventional family is no longer the norm but the idea of conventional family life is powerful. People expect it to bring them happiness but, in reality, it can be stressful.
- In Oakley's view, some groups, particularly among the educated **middle class**, are exploring other ways of living – both in families and without them. Dual-worker and lone-parent families are increasing.
- However, norms are not changing across all social groups because conventional families are self-perpetuating over time – they set the pattern for the next generation of parents.

Power within Conjugal Relationships

- One way of studying the distribution of power in **conjugal relationships** is by examining financial decision-making. Young and Willmott (1973) identified an increase in shared decision-making, including financial decisions, within symmetrical families.
- Pahl (1989) found that more couples share decisions on household spending compared with 30 years ago. However, husbands are still likely to dominate decision-making.
- Sociologists see domestic violence as a form of power in which one family member attempts to control others.
- Some feminists link women's oppression to patriarchy (male power) within families.

> **Key Thinker**
>
> Ann Oakley (1982)

> **Key Point**
>
> In her analysis of the conventional family, Oakley (1982) drew on research carried out by other sociologists.

Oakley's feminist perspective on families is different from Young and Willmott's functionalist approach.

> **Key Words**
>
> conjugal roles
> segregated conjugal roles
> joint conjugal roles
> wage
> instrumental role
> expressive role
> integrated conjugal roles
> symmetrical family
> double shift
> new man
> conventional family
> middle class
> conjugal relationships

> **Quick Test**
>
> 1. Which research method did Young and Willmott use in their study of families?
> 2. Identify one difference between functionalist and feminist perspectives on conjugal roles.
> 3. Explain one difference between joint and segregated conjugal roles.

Changing Relationships Within Families

You must be able to:

- Explain changes in authority relationships between parents and children
- Discuss changes in people's relationships with their wider family
- Explain Young and Willmott's principle of stratified diffusion
- Outline contemporary family-related issues.

Changing Relationships Between Parents and Children

- During the 19th century, children's experiences varied according to their age, gender and social class. Poverty may have prevented many parents from sending their children to school.
- After the introduction of the Education Act 1918, all children had to attend school until the age of 14. Young and Willmott argue that **childhood** was officially recognised as a separate stage in human life at this point.

Contemporary Parent–Child Relationships

- One view is that relationships are now less authoritarian and there is more emphasis on children's rights. Research suggests that middle-class families are more likely than working-class families to involve their children in decisions.
- Relationships are generally more child-centred and focus on children's needs. The average family size is smaller today than 100 years ago, so children get more individual attention from their parents.
- Young people are now financially dependent on their family for a longer period of time. This can potentially lead to conflict within families.
- Some children contribute to childcare and housework, help out in family businesses and provide emotional support.

People's Relationships with their Wider Family

- Some sociologists suggest that the wider family is becoming less important and family ties are weakening.
- Young and Willmott (1957) found that the extended family flourished in Bethnal Green in London during the mid-1950s and family ties were strong. However, in later research, they discovered that the nuclear family had become more isolated from the extended family.
- One view is that increasing **geographical mobility** and women's involvement in full-time paid work mean that family members see each other less often.
- An alternative view is that geographical distance affects the type of support between family members but does not eliminate it altogether. Support at a distance takes the form of visits, phone calls and financial help.

Geographical separation does not necessarily eliminate support between family members.

The Principle of Stratified Diffusion

- Young and Willmott (1973) developed the **principle of stratified diffusion** as a guide to changes in family life.
- According to this principle, many social changes (for example, in values and attitudes) start at the top of the social class system and work downwards. Changes in family life filter down from the middle class into the **working class**.

Contemporary Family-Related Issues

The Quality of Parenting

- The quality of parenting is one of the main factors affecting children's well-being.
- Research suggests that the quality of parent–child relationships is associated with children's educational achievements. Children's reading ability is linked to the reading environment around them.
- The quality of parent–child relationships is also associated with children's social skills and their relationships with peers. Parental warmth, lack of conflict and parental control seem important in developing children's social skills.

Relationships between Teenagers and Adults

- One view is that some parents cannot control their teenage children, and delinquent teenagers have been inadequately socialised into society's norms and values by their parents.
- Another concern is that a minority of teenagers are themselves parents.

Care of Elderly People

- **Life expectancy** has increased and the UK has an **ageing population**. Some people, particularly women, care for family members from different generations.
- Older people are often seen as **dependent family members**. However, research indicates that an older person's social class, gender and ethnicity affect their independence.

Arranged Marriage

- A marriage may be built on mutual attraction between two partners and it may also be arranged. An **arranged marriage** is based on consent and the partners' right to choose.
- It is important not to confuse arranged and forced marriage. In a forced marriage, one or both partners withhold their consent but the wedding still goes ahead. Forced marriages are illegal in Britain and forcing someone to marry can result in imprisonment.

> ### Quick Test
>
> 1. Young and Willmott (1973) study the family from a feminist perspective. True or false?
> 2. Identify one difference between an arranged and a forced marriage.
> 3. What is meant by life expectancy?

> ### Key Point
>
> Young and Willmott (1973) are key thinkers, so it is important that you understand their work on the symmetrical family and the principle of stratified diffusion.

> ### Key Words
>
> childhood
> geographical mobility
> principle of stratified diffusion
> working class
> life expectancy
> ageing population
> dependent family members
> arranged marriage

Changing Family and Household Structures

You must be able to:

- Describe and explain changes in family and household structures
- Describe and explain changes in patterns of fertility.

Changes in Family and Household Structures

- Since the mid-1970s, there have been significant changes in family and household structures. These include:
  - a decrease in the proportion of children living in conventional nuclear families headed by a married couple
  - an increase in the proportion of children living in families headed by a cohabiting couple
  - an increase in families headed by a same-sex couple
  - a significant increase in one-person households.

The Decrease in Reconstituted Families

- The number of reconstituted or **blended families** in England and Wales fell from 631 000 to 544 000 between 2001 and 2011, according to census data (Office for National Statistics).
- One reason for the decrease is that the average age at which women have their first baby is increasing. Babies are now more likely to be born to older couples, who are less likely to separate. This may reduce the chances that the babies will become step-children later on.
- Lone parents may be more likely to make up one half of a couple who live apart. 'Living apart together' relationships (the partners are in a committed relationship but live apart, because, for example, they work in different cities) do not count as blended families in the census data.

The Increase in Dual-Career Families

- As a result of the increasing proportion of married or cohabiting women in employment, there are more **dual-career families**.
- Some people (particularly women) may experience **role conflict** if the demands of their roles as a parent and an employee (or employer) clash.

The Increase in Lone-Parent Families

- The proportion of dependent children living with one parent in the UK has increased markedly since the 1970s. More recently, the proportion has remained fairly stable.
- The rise in lone-parent families is linked to the increase in divorce.
- The increase is also related to changing views on the family and marriage.
  - People now have more freedom of choice in their relationships.

> **Key Point**
>
> The functionalist perspective sees the decline in conventional nuclear families as a problem for society.

Women in dual-career families may experience role conflict.

- It is now more socially acceptable for single women to have children without a partner (for example, to become single mothers by choice through sperm donation).
- Some commentators link the rise in fatherless families to a decline in society's moral fibre and a **culture of dependency**. They see fatherless families as part of an **underclass** that depends on **welfare state** provision.

The Increase in One-person Households

- Over the last 30 years, the number of one-person households in the UK has increased significantly.
- This increase is partly due to the changing age structure of the population. People are living longer so there are more elderly, one-person households that typically contain widows.
- The growth is also linked to the increase in solo living among younger people. These households may comprise single people, divorcees, international migrants and people who 'live apart together'.

Changes in Patterns of Fertility

- The term fertility refers to the average number of children that women of childbearing age give birth to in a particular society.
- Women born in the UK are having fewer children (and at a later age) than 30 years ago. So there is a trend towards smaller families.

Reasons for the Changing Patterns of Fertility

- **Economic factors:** during the 19th century, childrearing among poor families was motivated partly by economic factors. This is no longer the case today.
- **Labour market uncertainty:** during global recessions when there is uncertainty about the job market, people may delay having children.
- **Later marriage:** the trend since the 1970s is for people to get married at an older age. Some women who marry later will also delay having children.
- **Women's increased participation in higher education and paid employment:** females have more options in addition to (or instead of) motherhood today.
- **Effective birth control methods:** women now have greater control over their fertility.

> ### Key Point
>
> Some approaches such as functionalism see the changes in family and household structures as a problem for society. Other sociologists see them as part of a move towards greater freedom of choice in relationships.

Quick Test

1. Since the 1970s, has the proportion of children living in conventional nuclear families headed by a married couple increased or decreased?
2. Identify one reason for the increase in lone-parent families since the 1970s.
3. Family size has increased, on average. True or false?

Key Words

blended families
dual-career families
role conflict
culture of dependency
underclass
welfare state

Marriage and Divorce

You must be able to:

- Describe different forms of marriage
- Outline the changing patterns of marriage in the UK
- Outline and explain the changing patterns of divorce
- Explain the consequences of divorce.

Different Forms of Marriage

Monogamy	In the UK, marriage is based on monogamy – being married to just one person at a time.
Bigamy	Marrying when already married to someone else – a criminal offence.
Serial monogamy	When a divorced person enters into a second marriage, then divorces, remarries, divorces, remarries, and so on.
Polygamy	The practice of having more than one spouse at the same time.
Polygyny	When a man has two or more wives at once.
Polyandry	When a woman has two or more husbands at once.

Changing Patterns of Marriage in the UK

The Decline in the Annual Number of Marriages

- The number of marriages in the UK peaked in 1972 at 480 000. Since then, the overall number has fallen, and in 2011 just over 286 600 marriages took place.

People are Getting Married Later

- Compared with the early 1970s, people now put off marriage until they are older. This is linked to increased educational and employment opportunities, particularly for women.
- It is also related to changing attitudes towards premarital sex, which is now generally considered more acceptable.

The Introduction of Civil Partnerships and Same-Sex Marriages

- Since 2005 in the UK, same-sex couples aged 16 years and over can have their relationship legally recognised as a civil partnership.
- Marriages of same-sex couples were introduced in 2014.

The Increase in Cohabitation

- The proportion of people cohabiting in Britain has more or less doubled over the last 20 years.
- This increase is linked to changing social attitudes towards sex outside marriage. Before the 1960s, it was seen as unacceptable for unmarried women to be sexually active.
- The secularisation process has weakened the religious barrier to cohabitation: living together is much less likely to be seen as 'living in sin' compared to the 1940s.
- The high cost of weddings may also put people off marriage.

> **Key Point**
>
> There is global diversity in the forms of marriage.

The Increase in Births outside Marriage

- During the 1960s and 1970s, the number of births outside marriage in the UK increased. However, many of these babies were born to cohabiting couples.
- Births outside marriage are no longer stigmatised.

Changing Patterns of Divorce

- A divorce is the legal ending of a marriage. In general, the number of divorces per year in England and Wales has risen since 1945, although there have also been decreases. The number peaked in 1993.
- Statistics on divorce reveal nothing about the extent of empty shell marriages.

Reasons for the Increase in Divorce

- Legal changes have made divorces cheaper and quicker to obtain.
- Changing attitudes since the 1960s mean that divorce is now more socially acceptable.
- The secularisation process has weakened the religious barrier to divorce.
- Women in unhappy marriages are less tied to their husbands through economic dependence.
- The media's emphasis on 'romantic love' encourages couples to have high **expectations** of marriage. If these expectations are not met, it may result in an increase in divorce.

The Consequences of Divorce for Individuals and Society

- Rising divorce rates have contributed to an increase in one-person households, and lone-parent and reconstituted families.
- Living in a reconstituted family may create problems for some family members who have to adjust to different expectations of behaviour. On the other hand, more people may be available to provide attention and support.
- Conflict between the former spouses may continue after they divorce due to disputes about parenting and property.
- Some children lose contact with a parent or with members of their extended family following their parents' divorce.
- Divorced people, particularly men, may experience loss of emotional support if their friends and social networks change.
- Divorce can lead to loss of income for the former partners. After divorce, lone-parent families with dependent children may face financial hardship.

Divorce is now more socially acceptable compared to the 1960s and some people throw divorce parties today.

> **Key Point**
>
> The functionalist perspective sees some of the social changes described here as having negative consequences for individuals and for society.

> **Key Words**
>
> monogamy
> bigamy
> serial monogamy
> polygamy
> polygyny
> **polyandry**
> cohabitation
> **changing social attitudes**
> secularisation
> **expectations**

> **Quick Test**
>
> 1. Polygamy describes the practice of having more than one wife at once. True or false?
> 2. Identify one reason for the increase in cohabitation in Britain over the last 20 years.
> 3. Identify one possible consequence of parental divorce for children.

The Sociological Approach

1   Describe what sociologists mean by a culture.   [3]

_____

_____

_____

_____

_____

_____

_____

2   Which term is commonly used by sociologists to describe beliefs and ideas about what is seen as worth striving for in society? Shade **one** box only.   [1]

A Norms ◯   **B** Values ◯   **C** Social issues ◯   **D** Social processes ◯

The Key Ideas of Marx and Durkheim

3   Describe the means of production as outlined by Karl Marx.   [3]

_____

_____

_____

_____

_____

Continue your answer on a separate piece of paper.

Other Sociological Approaches

4 Describe what sociologists mean by value consensus in society. [3]

_____

_____

_____

_____

_____

_____

Research Design

5 Describe a representative sample within the research process. [3]

_____

_____

_____

_____

_____

_____

6 Which term is used by sociologists to describe a sampling technique in which a researcher contacts one member of the population and identifies other members through them? Shade **one** box only. [1]

A Random sampling ○ **B** Quota sampling ○

C Snowball sampling ○ **D** Systematic sampling ○

Quantitative Methods

7 Which term is used by sociologists to describe a question that allows respondents to put forward their own answers? Shade **one** box only. [1]

A Leading question ○ **B** Open-ended question ○

C Closed question ○ **D** Pre-set question ○

Qualitative Methods

8 Identify and explain **one** advantage of using focus group interviews to investigate fear of crime within a local community. [4]

....

....

....

....

....

....

....

....

....

....

Secondary Sources of Data

9 Identify and explain **one** disadvantage of using police-recorded crime statistics to investigate domestic violence. [4]

....

....

....

....

....

....

....

....

....

....

Different Family Forms

1   Identify and describe **one** type of family in Britain today.   [3]

The Functions of Families

2   Which of the following is described by sociologists as a function of the family?
Shade **one** box only.   [1]

A   Marriage   ◯   **B**   Socialisation   ◯

C   Monogamy   ◯   **D**   Conjugal roles   ◯

The Marxist Perspective on Families

3   Describe the private sphere as outlined by Zaretsky.   [3]

....

....

....

....

....

Feminist and other Critical Views of Families

4 Describe canalisation within the socialisation process. [3]

....

....

....

....

....

....

....

Conjugal Role Relationships

5 Describe a symmetrical family. [3]

....

....

....

....

Changing Relationships Within Families

6 Describe the principle of stratified diffusion as outlined by Young and Willmott. [3]

Changing Family and Household Structures

7 Identify and explain **one** reason for the increase in lone-parent families since the 1970s. [4]

_____

Marriage and Divorce

8 Identify and explain **one** factor that may have led to an increase in the divorce rate since the 1970s.   [4]

_____

The Role of Education from a Functionalist Perspective

You must be able to:

- Explain the functions of education
- Describe and criticise Durkheim's key ideas on education
- Describe and criticise Parsons' key ideas on education.

Formal and Informal Education

- **Education** involves acquiring knowledge and learning new skills.
  - **Formal education** takes place in educational establishments such as schools and universities where people learn knowledge and skills across a wide range of subjects.
  - **Informal education** takes place when people develop knowledge and skills by observing what is happening around them in everyday life.

Functions of the Education System

Function	Why it is important
Serving the needs of the economy	Education has an economic role in teaching the knowledge and skills that future workers will need in a competitive global **economy**.
Facilitating **social mobility**	The education system enables people to move up (or down) the social ladder. Gifted students from disadvantaged backgrounds can achieve qualifications and move into a higher social class.
Fostering social cohesion	Through subjects such as **Citizenship**, students identify themselves as British citizens. Schools help to reinforce the 'glue' or the social bonds that unite different people in society.
Selection and role allocation	The education system works like a sieve, grading students and allocating them to jobs based on their individual merit, abilities and exam results.

> **Key Point**
>
> Functionalism focuses on the positive functions that the education system performs in society.

 Schools (like families) function as agencies of socialisation and social control.

> **Key Thinker**
>
> Durkheim (1858–1917)

Durkheim's Key Ideas on Education

- The main function of education is to transmit society's norms and values. Subjects like history instil shared norms and values, and encourage individual children to see themselves as part of society.
- Through the use of sanctions (or punishment) at school and by respecting the school rules, children learn to respect rules in general.
- In a complex industrial society, education equips children with the skills they will need for their future work roles.

Through history lessons, individual students learn society's norms and values and come to see themselves as part of the social group.

Criticisms of Durkheim

- Marxists argue that the education system transmits ideas that benefit the ruling class rather than society as a whole. Some feminists argue that schools transmit patriarchal culture.
- Some students accept neither the school's rules nor society's norms and values.
- The education system does not necessarily teach skills that prepare students for their future workplace roles.

Parsons' Key Ideas on Education

- The education system is the main agency of socialisation in modern society. It acts as the bridge between the family and society, and prepares children for their adult roles.
- Children have **ascribed status** in families and are judged according to **particularistic standards**. In society, however, status is achieved and people are judged according to **universalistic standards** that apply to everyone in the same way. The education system prepares children to enter the wider society by treating everyone in terms of universalistic standards and by operating on the basis of **achieved status**.
- Schools, as an agency of socialisation, promote two key values – achievement and equality of opportunity. These values are important in the wider society. Advanced industrial societies need a system of rewarding people differently based on their achievement. Having been through school, people accept this as fair, so long as there are equal opportunities.
- Role allocation: the education system matches individuals to their future jobs and status in society, based on their talents and abilities. In a **meritocracy**, the most able reach the top jobs.

Criticisms of Parsons

- Marxists argue that the education system transmits values that benefit the dominant groups in society.
- Some feminists question whether the education system is based on meritocracy and whether it provides equal opportunities.
- Critics question how far role allocation is effective or meritocratic. People with the best qualifications do not always get the top jobs.

Key Thinker

Talcott Parsons (1961)

Think about how Parsons makes connections between families and education.

Key Point

As we saw in Chapter 1 (pages 8–9) and Chapter 2 (pages 26–27), Durkheim and Parsons are key thinkers within functionalism. Make sure that you understand Durkheim's ideas about the function of education in transmitting norms and values, and Parsons' ideas about achieved status and meritocracy in schools.

Key Words

education
formal education
informal education
economy
social mobility
Citizenship
ascribed status
particularistic standards
universalistic standards
achieved status
meritocracy

Quick Test

1. Achieved status is fixed at birth. True or false?
2. Particularistic standards apply to everyone in the same way. True or false?

The Marxist Approach to Education

You must be able to:

- Describe the Marxist view of the role of education
- Describe the key ideas of Bowles and Gintis on education and capitalism
- Criticise the key ideas of Bowles and Gintis.

The Role of Education from a Marxist Perspective

What the education system does	Explanation
Serves the interests of the ruling class	By passing on ideas and beliefs that benefit the ruling class (for example, that capitalist society is fair and meritocratic), the education system serves ruling class interests.
Reproduces the class structure	Education appears to reward students fairly based on their individual abilities. However, it actually favours pupils from more privileged backgrounds. Over time, education reproduces (or recreates) the advantages that some social class groups have over others.
Breeds competition	Through exams and sport at school, students are encouraged to accept values such as **competition**. This helps to maintain capitalism, which is based on competition.
Secondary socialisation	Working-class students learn norms and values at schools that prepare them for their lower position in a capitalist society. For example, they learn to accept hierarchy at school and to obey rules.

Key Point

Marxist approaches examine the relationship between education and capitalism.

Marxists argue that schools breed competition and, in doing so, help to maintain capitalism.

The Key Ideas of Bowles and Gintis

- The main role of the education system is to reproduce (recreate over time) a workforce with the necessary qualities to meet the needs of the capitalist economy. These qualities include being hard-working, disciplined, obedient and reluctant to question authority.
- Schools reward students who display these qualities with high grades. Students who show greater independence and creative thinking are more likely to get lower grades. Schools produce an unimaginative and unquestioning workforce with the necessary attitudes for exploitation.

Key Thinkers

Bowles and Gintis (1976)

- The education system helps to produce a workforce for capitalism mainly through the way schooling is structured and the **hidden curriculum**.
- Bowles and Gintis use the term **correspondence principle** to describe the way education and work connect or fit together (correspond) in capitalist society.

Bowles and Gintis's Correspondence Principle	
School and its Hidden Curriculum	**Workplace**
There is a rigid hierarchy of authority with coercive relationships, rules and discipline.	There is a rigid hierarchy of authority with rules and discipline.
The **curriculum** is fragmented or divided into little packages of knowledge.	Jobs (for example, in car manufacturing) are broken down into separate tasks.
Tasks are mundane or boring.	Tasks are mundane.
Students lack power over what they learn.	Workers have minimum control over work tasks.
Schoolwork is a means to an end (qualifications) rather than an end in itself (satisfaction).	Work is a means to an end (pay) rather than an end in itself (job satisfaction).

- Bowles and Gintis see meritocracy as a myth. Students' social class background rather than their **intelligence quotient** (IQ) is the most important influence on their educational achievements.

Criticisms of Bowles and Gintis
- Bowles and Gintis assume that students passively accept the values taught via the hidden curriculum. However, many students reject the values of the school and resist their teachers' authority (see pages 62–63 on Willis).
- Bowles and Gintis exaggerate the power of the education system in forming personalities and attitudes.
- Businesses today require creative, independent workers rather than passive, unthinking workers. Many teaching methods now encourage creativity rather than rote learning.
- Functionalist approaches see the education system as based on meritocracy and equality of opportunity.

Bowles and Gintis argue that education creates a passive, obedient workforce to meet the needs of capitalism.

> **Key Point**
>
> Bowles and Gintis (1976) are key thinkers who studied schooling in America from a Marxist perspective. It is important that you are familiar with their ideas on education and the correspondence principle. In their methods, they drew on data from their study of 237 New York high school students, statistical data and historical studies of schooling in America.

> **Quick Test**
>
> 1. Identify one difference between Marxist and functionalist approaches to education.
> 2. What term do sociologists use to describe the things learnt in school (such as valuing punctuality or obedience) that are not formally taught in lessons?
> 3. What term describes a score based on a test designed to measure a person's intelligence?

> **Key Words**
>
> competition
> hidden curriculum
> correspondence principle
> curriculum
> intelligence quotient

Different Types of School

You must be able to:

- Identify and describe different types of school such as primary and secondary, state and private
- Describe alternative forms of educational provision such as deschooling.

The Structure of the Education System

Early years education	State nursery schools and nursery classes in primary schools, for example, offer free, part-time provision for children aged 3–4.
Primary education	Most state primary schools cater for girls and boys aged 5–11.
Secondary education	Secondary schools include **comprehensive schools**, **special schools**, **free schools** and **academies**. Most cater for students aged 11–16.
Further education (FE)	**Further education** mainly caters for students aged 16 years and over. Courses are usually provided by sixth form and FE colleges.
Higher education (HE)	The **higher education** sector includes universities that provide higher level academic and vocational courses (such as degrees).

The Independent Sector

- The independent sector refers to **fee paying schools**. It is made up of **private schools** (all fee charging schools) and **public schools** (older independent schools, such as Eton and Rugby).
- Around seven per cent of schoolchildren in England attend **independent schools**.

← Think about how the functionalist and Marxist approaches might view the private sector in education.

Advantages of Independent Schools

- They usually have a lower teacher–student ratio than state schools so students receive more individual attention during lessons.
- Resources and facilities are often better than in state schools.
- Many are **selective schools** and their **ethos** stresses academic achievement. Exam results tend to be above the national average.
- Parents' input is high in terms of fees, support and expectations.

State Schools

- State schools are not based on parents' ability to pay fees.
- The intake is more socially mixed (for example, in social class terms) than independent schools.
- State schools may provide a route of upward social mobility for students from low income families.
- Students do not have to travel far to attend a local state school.

> **Key Point**
>
> Critics argue that the private sector maintains the privileges of the rich. Supporters argue that people have the right to choose between state and private education.

The Tripartite System

- The 1944 Education Act set up the **tripartite system**. It aimed to provide children with a free, state education based on their individual abilities. School allocation was based on the results of the **11-plus** examination. Children attended one of three types of school (secondary modern, secondary technical and grammar) according to their aptitudes and needs.
- Some local authorities such as Dorset still have grammar schools, with admission based on an entrance exam.

Advantages of the Comprehensive System Compared to the Tripartite System

- Comprehensive schools are designed to cater for children of all abilities. There is no entrance exam so nobody is labelled a 'failure'.
- Children from different social classes attend the same school, which breaks down social barriers.
- Comprehensives are usually large, so more subjects and facilities are available.

Problems with the Comprehensive System

- Critics argue the following.
  - Comprehensives limit parental choice. Students are expected to attend their closest school, regardless of its reputation. ←
  - Academic students are held back academically in **mixed-ability** groups.
  - Academic working-class children will achieve more at a grammar than a comprehensive school.
- Supporters argue that the principle of comprehensive education has not been achieved because comprehensives do not have mixed intakes, e.g. a suburban school's intake is usually middle class. Also, most comprehensive schools are not fully comprehensive because, for instance, they have **setting** in particular subjects.

Alternative Educational Provision

- With **home tuition** or home schooling, children are taught at home by parents or tutors rather than in schools. There are concerns, however, about the standards of home tuition and its impact on children's social development.
- Illich (1995) argues that schools repress children and promote passive conformity. He supports **deschooling** and argues that education in its current form should be abolished. Instead, people should set up learning webs, decide what to learn and go about it in creative and exploratory ways.

> ### Key Point
>
> State schools are publicly funded, for example through local councils or government. Most state schools must follow the national curriculum. Independent schools charge fees and do not have to follow the national curriculum.

The issue of grammar schools is still hotly debated among politicians today. Under Theresa May, the Conservative Prime Minister, grammar schools were a key part of education policy in 2017. By contrast, the Labour Party opposes grammar schools.

> ### Key Words
>
> comprehensive schools
> special schools
> free schools
> academies
> further education
> higher education
> fee paying schools
> private schools
> public schools
> independent schools
> selective schools
> ethos
> tripartite system
> 11-plus (eleven plus)
> mixed ability
> setting
> home tuition
> deschooling

> ### Quick Test
>
> 1. Academies are funded directly by government. True or false?
> 2. Comprehensive schools are selective. True or false?
> 3. Identify one difference between a private school and a public school.

Social Class and Educational Achievement

You must be able to:

- Explain how social class affects educational achievement
- Describe Halsey's key ideas on class-based inequalities
- Describe Ball's key ideas on parental choice and competition between schools.

Patterns of Educational Achievement Based on Class

- In general, middle-class students achieve better results in **public examinations** than working-class students. They are also more likely to study in higher education.

Halsey: Origins and Destinations

- Halsey, Heath and Ridge (1980) examined the social class origins and educational destinations of a large sample of men. Respondents' social class was based on their father's occupation and they were divided into three groups:
  - the service class (for example, higher-grade professionals)
  - the intermediate class (for example, clerical workers)
  - the working class (for example, manual workers in industry).
- Halsey *et al.* found evidence of social class inequalities in education. A boy from the service class, compared to a working-class boy, was four times more likely to be at school at 16, eight times more likely at 17, and 10 times more likely at 18. He was 11 times more likely to go to university than a working-class boy.

Explanations for Class-based Differences in Achievement

- Explanations for social class differences in **achievement** focus on home factors, school factors (see pages 56–57) and the impact of government reforms.

Economic Circumstances and Material Deprivation

- Poor housing and overcrowding adversely affect performance at school. Working-class children are more likely to experience these conditions.
- Students from affluent backgrounds are more likely to have facilities (such as computers and quiet spaces) to help them study at home.
- Many middle-class parents can afford private tuition and property in the catchment areas of good schools.

Key Thinkers

Halsey, Heath and Ridge (1980)

Key Point

Key thinkers Halsey, Heath and Ridge (1980) drew on data from a face-to-face survey of men born between 1913 and 1952 and educated in England and Wales.

Parental Values and Expectations

- Parents in professional occupations often value educational achievement and expect their children to do well at school. Some working-class people may not particularly value education and achieving a high occupational status.
- Working-class children may have less parental interest, support and encouragement than middle-class children.

Cultural Deprivation

- **Cultural deprivation** theories suggest that the sub-culture of some low income groups inhibits educational achievement. Working-class children's home environment may not provide them with the cultural resources and educational experiences (such as family visits to museums or libraries) to perform well at school.

Cultural Capital

- Middle-class parents have the right sort of **cultural capital** to help their children succeed in schools. They know how the education system works and how to work it to their advantage.
- Well-qualified parents are better equipped to help with homework and monitor progress.

Some parents are better qualified than others to help with homework.

Ball, Bowe and Gewirtz: The Impact of Market Forces on Parental Choice

- Ball *et al.* focus on the effects that parental choice and competition between schools has on the education system, in particular whether it leads to greater inequality.
- With the publication of examination **league tables**, schools want to attract 'motivated' parents and 'able' children. More resources are directed towards students who are likely to perform well in examinations.
- Middle-class parents are more likely to know how to deal with secondary school choices. Working-class parents are more likely to prefer to send their children to local schools.
- Material resources bring advantages in the market place. For example, parents with their own transport have a wider choice of schools.
- Having the right sort of cultural capital helps parents to play the market. It brings knowledge of the education system and confidence in how to work it.
- Ball *et al.* argue that **marketisation** and **educational reform** reinforce the advantages of middle-class parents and make education less equal. Schools are now more concerned with attracting gifted and advantaged students than with helping disadvantaged ones.

Key Thinkers

Ball, Bowe and Gewirtz (1994)

Key Point

Ball, Bowe and Gewirtz (1994) interviewed staff and governors in 15 secondary schools, as well as primary school heads and parents of primary school children. They also drew on secondary sources of data.

Key Words

public examinations
achievement
cultural deprivation
cultural capital
league tables
marketisation
educational reform

> **Quick Test**
>
> 1. Material deprivation refers to cultural rather than financial issues. True or false?
> 2. Marketisation refers to the policy of bringing market forces (such as competition and choice) into education. True or false?

The Impact of School Processes on Working-Class Students' Achievements

You must be able to:

- Describe interactionist perspectives on education
- Explain how processes such as streaming, setting, mixed-ability teaching, labelling and the self-fulfilling prophecy affect the achievement of working-class students
- Describe the key ideas of Ball on teacher expectations.

Interactionist Perspectives on Education

- **Interactionism** focuses on small-scale interactions between individuals, such as teachers and students in classrooms. Research suggests that teachers classify students into types based on factors such as their appearance, ability and how conformist they are. Once particular students are judged as deviant types, it is difficult for their behaviour to be seen positively.
- Some teachers label students on the basis of their social class rather than their ability. Labelling theory suggests that labels are sticky. Once a label is attached to a student, they may come to see themselves in terms of the label and behave accordingly. Other people may see them in terms of the label.
- Negative **labelling** of working-class students (for example, as unlikely to do well in maths) can lead to a **self-fulfilling prophecy**. In this case, students perform as badly or as well as their teachers expect them to.

Interactionists study the interaction between teachers and students in classrooms.

Effects of Streaming and Setting

- With streaming, students are allocated to a class based on their general ability and are taught in this class for most subjects. With setting, students are allocated to classes based on their attainment in particular subjects such as English.
- Research suggests that streaming is often linked to social class. A disproportionately higher number of lower-stream students are drawn from the working class.
- Streaming and setting may have unintended effects. If the confidence of students in the lower streams or sets is damaged, they may not try to improve. Teachers may give less attention and encouragement to students in the lower streams. Some commentators see mixed-ability teaching as more fair than streaming.

> **Key Point**
>
> When explaining working-class educational underachievement, it is important to focus on home factors, school factors and the impact of educational reforms.

Ball: Banding and Teacher Expectations

- Stephen Ball (1981) undertook a **case study** of a mixed comprehensive school and examined the way it was organised.
- In the banding system, students were placed into one of three bands (similar to streaming). Band 1 contained the most able students and band 3 contained the least able. Although placement was supposed to be based on test scores, in practice, banding did not necessarily operate on ability. In cases where students had similar abilities, those whose fathers were not manual workers were more likely to be put in band 1.
- Some students' behaviour changed over time as a result of the bands they were placed in. Ball linked this to **teacher expectations** of each band. For example, teachers expected band 1 students to be well behaved and hard-working, and band 2 students to be difficult and uncooperative. This led to a gradual change in the behaviour of band 2 students to mirror their teachers' expectations.
- Each band was taught differently and followed different educational routes. Students in band 1 were encouraged to have high aspirations and to study academic courses. Students in band 2 were steered towards more practical subjects and lower-level examinations.
- With the introduction of mixed-ability groups at the school, students were less obviously polarised (or divided into two contrasting groups). Teachers, however, continued to label middle-class students as the most able and cooperative. This labelling was reflected in exam results.

Pupil Cultures

- Research suggests that streaming can lead to the development of an **anti-school sub-culture** that opposes the school's learning objectives.
- In response to being labelled as 'failures', some lower stream students reject the school's academic values and rules. Instead, they develop a sub-culture that stresses defiance of teachers and authority.
- This provides them with an alternative source of status among their peers.

Paul Willis also studied the creation of a counter-school culture (see pages 62–63).

Revise

Key Thinker

Stephen Ball (1981)

Key Point

Ball used participant observation: he observed lessons and taught some classes. He interviewed students and teachers, and carried out small-scale questionnaires. He also analysed secondary sources such as school records and registers.

Key Words

interactionism
labelling
self-fulfilling prophecy
case study
teacher expectations
anti-school sub-culture

Quick Test

1. What do interactionists focus on when exploring educational achievement?
2. Identify one secondary source of data that Ball used.
3. Identify one possible consequence of banding.

Ethnicity and Educational Achievement

You must be able to:

- Explain how home factors can affect the achievement of different ethnic groups
- Explain how school factors can affect achievement
- Explain how government reforms can impact on achievement.

Patterns of Achievement

- Generally, students from some minority ethnic groups (such as Chinese and Indian) achieve better results in public examinations than others (such as Black Caribbean and Pakistani groups).
- Some of the differences in achievement between ethnic groups may reflect social class differences.
- White working-class boys achieve the lowest GCSE grades compared to other ethnic groups.

Home Factors

- **Material deprivation:** students from some minority ethnic groups (such as Bangladeshi and Black Caribbean) are more likely to experience material deprivation than white British pupils. Economic circumstances can affect achievement.
- **Cultural factors:** schools are seen as institutions in which white, 'mainstream' norms and values dominate. As a result, students from some minority ethnic backgrounds may be at a disadvantage.
- **Parental values:** research suggests that British Chinese parents value education and that, in Chinese culture, children respect older people. So British Chinese students develop high educational aspirations and get positive self-esteem from being 'good students'.

Look out for links between the topics of education and families.

- **Cultural capital:** white, educated, middle-class parents are likely to have the right kind of cultural capital. They may draw on their own learning, for example, to help with homework. Their knowledge of the education system places their children at an advantage. Parents who were educated outside the UK may not be able to support their children to the same extent.

Some parents' cultural capital gives them the confidence and knowledge to work the system.

School Factors

- Type of school attended: research suggests that the main factor in explaining differences in educational attainment is the school attended. The quality of teaching, resources available and equal opportunities policies within the school can influence achievement. Some sociologists argue that minority ethnic students who attend good schools do as well as other students in these schools.

- Teacher expectations and labelling: some teachers may have different expectations of students based on their ethnic origin. For example, teachers may have high expectations of Chinese students, who are seen as capable and hard-working, and low expectations of Black Caribbean students. Teachers' labels may lead to a self-fulfilling prophecy which affects students' educational attainments.
- An **ethnocentric curriculum**: one view is that the **formal curriculum** is ethnocentric (biased towards white, European culture). The national curriculum, for example, generally ignores non-European languages, literature, art and music. Subjects like history, for instance, may be taught from a British or European perspective. If students feel undervalued at school, this may lead to underachievement.
- School culture: critics argue that schools are dominated by a white, mainstream culture. Aspects of school life may affect the achievements of some minority ethnic students. For example, expectations about clothing may not take into account some minority cultures' norms and values.
- **Institutional racism** occurs when an organisation fails to provide an appropriate service to people because of their ethnic origin, culture or colour. Institutional racism is an unintended consequence of the way institutions such as schools are organised. The relatively high rate of fixed-term **exclusion** of students from Black Caribbean backgrounds, for example, has been linked to institutional racism.

Government Policies

- Legislation such as the Equality Act makes it illegal for educational providers to discriminate on the basis of **ethnicity**.
- If a school's admissions policy gives it scope to select its intake, some minority ethnic and working-class students may be disadvantaged.
- The emphasis on marketisation, parental choice and competition between schools to raise standards may have made life more difficult for some urban schools with an intake of minority ethnic (or working-class) students.

> **Key Point**
>
> Educational reforms and classroom practices may have unintended consequences.

> **Key Point**
>
> When discussing the underachievement of students from some minority ethnic groups, it is important to discuss home-based factors, school-based factors and educational reforms.

Look out for links between explanations of the underachievement of students from working-class and minority ethnic backgrounds.

> **Quick Test**
>
> 1. What term describes a curriculum based on white European culture?
> 2. Identify one possible reason for the relatively high rates of exclusion among students from Black Caribbean backgrounds.
> 3. Identify one home factor that could explain the underachievement of some minority ethnic students.

> **Key Words**
>
> ethnocentric curriculum
> formal curriculum
> institutional racism
> exclusion
> ethnicity

Gender and Educational Achievement

You must be able to:

- Describe the patterns of achievement based on gender
- Explain the improvements in girls' educational achievement
- Explain the reasons for boys' educational underachievement.

Patterns of Educational Achievement

- Traditionally, boys got better results at A Level than girls.
  - Towards the end of the 1980s, this gender gap in achievement began to narrow.
  - By the early 2000s, girls were doing better than boys at both GCSE and A Level.
  - However, results at A Level in 2014 suggest that the gender gap has started to narrow again following the introduction of end-of-course examinations. ← Bear in mind that most GCSEs and A Levels no longer include coursework assessment.
- Differences in subject choice remain. Girls are more likely to choose subjects such as English and Art and Design at A Level and boys are more likely to choose physics and maths.
- This affects students' choices within higher education and their future careers.
- Some sociologists link this to the **gendered curriculum**: some subjects (including high status subjects such as maths and science) are associated with masculinity and others (such as languages and humanities) are associated with femininity.
- Not all students who are male, working class or from a minority ethnic background underachieve. For example, boys from schools in very affluent areas generally perform better than boys and girls from schools in very deprived areas.

> **Key Point**
>
> Sociologists argue that gender, class and ethnicity combine to influence a person's educational achievement.

Explanations for the Improvements in Girls' Achievements

- Feminism has changed attitudes towards gender roles. In the past, males were usually expected to be breadwinners while females were expected to be homemakers. Today, girls are more focused on paid employment and financial independence, and see educational success as a route to these. ← Think about how the idea of breadwinner and homemaker roles links to functionalist accounts of the nuclear family.
- Laws such as the Sex Discrimination Act (1975) and the Equality Act (2010) have made gender discrimination in education illegal.
- Many schools have introduced equal opportunities policies to address inequality and change classroom practices.
- The National Curriculum provides girls and boys with equal access to the same subjects. Students can no longer opt out of subjects such as science at GCSE.
- Some feminists, however, argue that the educational system remains patriarchal. For example, girls still experience sexism in schools and men are still more likely than women to become secondary school heads.

Females see educational success as a route to a career and financial independence.

Reasons for Boys' Underachievement

- Although achievement levels for males are increasing overall, male students appear to be underperforming compared to female students.
- One explanation focuses on the feminisation of primary schooling. The majority of primary school teachers are female and there are not enough male teachers to act as role models to reduce macho or 'laddish' behaviour among boys.
- A related view is that schools have become too 'girl friendly' or biased towards females. Boys are forced to learn in ways that do not suit them. This includes an emphasis on verbal skills, coursework and a non-competitive environment rather than on practical skills.
- Some sociologists argue that boys and men are experiencing a **crisis of masculinity**. Males see their traditional masculine identity as under threat and believe they no longer have a clear-cut role in society. This can impact on boys' self-esteem and motivation at school.
- Some students (particularly males) may experience peer pressure to conform to the norms of an 'urban' or 'street' culture that does not value education.
- 'Laddish' cultures may emphasise that it is 'uncool' to work hard. This peer culture may encourage anti-learning attitudes and affect the progress of particular boys (and girls) in some schools. However, among schools in middle-class neighbourhoods, boys may not see education as 'uncool'. They may achieve status among their peers by displaying academic abilities.
- Some teachers may have lower expectations of male students who they tend to see as lacking in motivation. This labelling may lead to a self-fulfilling prophecy.

> ## Key Point
>
> Some commentators see the concern with male underachievement in education as part of a **moral panic** fuelled by the media.

Reasons for Gender Differences in Subject Choice

Type of factor	Explanation
Home-based	Gender socialisation within the home; e.g. if boys have more experience of science-related toys outside school, this could encourage them to see science as a 'male' subject.
School-based	Gender stereotyping in textbooks, teacher attitudes to gender, the gendered curriculum and socialisation in schools.

> ## Quick Test
>
> 1. Identify one reason for the improvement in girls' educational achievements.
> 2. A moral panic usually involves a media-fuelled over-reaction to a social group. True or false?
> 3. Identify one reason why girls and boys tend to choose different subjects at A Level.

> ## Key Words
>
> gendered curriculum
> crisis of masculinity
> moral panic

Perspectives on the Counter-School Culture

You must be able to:

- Explain Willis's ideas on the counter-school culture
- Criticise Willis's account.

Willis and the Counter-School Culture

Key Thinker

Paul Willis (1977)

- Paul Willis (1977) carried out an ethnographic case study of 12 working-class boys in a single-sex secondary modern school on a council estate in the Midlands.
- He used several qualitative methods including observation and participant observation in the school, group discussions, informal interviews and diaries.
- Willis explored the **counter-school culture** of the 12 'lads' during their last 18 months at school.
- This culture involved resisting the school, its teachers and their authority. The lads focused on 'dossing' and 'having a laff'. They saw the more conformist boys at school (the 'ear'oles') as 'cissies'.
- The values of the counter-school culture stressed masculinity and toughness, not being a 'cissy', and being able to handle oneself.
- The 'lads' rejected the mental work involved in learning, which they viewed as unmanly. They saw manual work as real work for men and **white-collar work** as 'effeminate'.
- Willis followed the lads as they moved from school to work and observed them during their first six months in working-class jobs such as fitting tyres, laying carpets and working as plumbers' mates.
- He argues that the counter-school culture prepares them for working-class jobs and the shop-floor culture.
- Willis shows how working-class boys end up in working-class jobs in a capitalist economy. The boys' counter-school practices contribute towards them getting working-class jobs. In this way, the class structure is reproduced over time.

Willis found that smoking and drinking were important within the counter-school culture.

Education and Capitalism

- Willis's ideas on the relationship between education and capitalism are different from those of Bowles and Gintis (who are also Marxists). Bowles and Gintis discuss the correspondence principle and highlight the way education and work correspond or fit together under capitalism (see pages 50–51). They see schools as turning working-class students into passive and conformist workers for capitalism.

Key Point

Paul Willis (1977) is a key Marxist thinker in the sociology of education. It is important that you are familiar with his work on the counter-school culture and his methods of research.

- In Willis's view, however, education does not socialise the lads into becoming passive and docile workers for capitalism. The lads challenged authority figures at school on a daily basis.
- Willis emphasises the workings of the counter-school culture rather than the power of the education system in the socialisation process in explaining why working-class students end up in working-class jobs.

Key Point

From a Marxist perspective, Willis sees the education system as serving capitalism. From an interactionist approach, he explores the interaction between teachers and students at school and how the boys make sense of their experiences of schooling.

The counter-school culture may prepare working-class boys for working-class jobs.

Criticisms of Willis

- Feminists argue that Willis ignores the experiences of girls in schools and celebrates lad culture.
- Other critics argue that Willis does not explore the conformist boys' experiences of education or their views on the lads.
- Functionalists see education as teaching knowledge and skills and as linked to role allocation based on equality of opportunity and meritocracy.
- Given the small sample size, it is not possible to generalise from the findings.
- Willis's ideas may not be relevant today because there are far fewer manual working-class jobs available for school leavers.

You can draw on Willis's study when discussing school processes and anti-school sub-cultures (see pages 56–57).

Quick Test

1. Identify one way in which a counter-school culture might influence students' educational achievements.
2. Identify one difference between the views of Bowles and Gintis and those of Willis.
3. White-collar work involves skilled, semi-skilled or unskilled manual work and is performed by blue-collar workers. True or false?

Key Words

counter-school culture
white-collar work

Different Family Forms

1 Describe family diversity in British society today. [3]

The Functions of Families

2 Identify and explain **one** function of families. [4]

The Marxist Perspective on Families

3 Describe the public sphere as outlined by Zaretsky. [3]

Feminist and Other Critical Views on Families

4 Which term is used by sociologists to describe a family in which power is held by a woman?
Shade **one** box only. [1]

A   Patriarchal family   ◯

B   Matriarchal family   ◯

C   Conventional family   ◯

D   Same-sex family   ◯

Conjugal Role Relationships

5 Describe the expressive role within the nuclear family. [3]

_____

_____

_____

_____

_____

_____

Changing Relationships Within Families

6 Identify and explain **one** way in which relationships between parents and children have changed over the last 100 years. [4]

_____

_____

_____

_____

_____

_____

_____

Changing Family and Household Structures

7 Describe **one** example of role conflict [3]

Marriage and Divorce

8 Describe the secularisation process. [3]

The Role of Education from a Functionalist Perspective

1   Describe **one** feature of a meritocratic society.   [3]

_____

_____

_____

_____

_____

_____

The Marxist Approach to Education

2   Describe **one** aspect of the hidden curriculum in schools.   [3]

_____

_____

_____

_____

_____

_____

_____

Different Types of School

3 Which term describes a type of school that selects its intake based on ability? Shade **one** box only. [1]

A Grammar school ◯   **C** Academy ◯

B Comprehensive school ◯   **D** Free school ◯

Social Class and Educational Achievement

4 Describe marketisation in education. [3]

....

....

....

....

....

....

....

The Impact of School Processes on Working-Class Students' Achievements

5 Describe **one** school-based factor that could influence students' performance. [3]

....

....

....

....

_____

_____

_____

_____

Ethnicity and Educational Achievement

6 Describe the ethnocentric curriculum in education. [3]

_____

_____

_____

_____

_____

_____

_____

_____

Gender and Educational Achievement

7 Identify and explain **one** reason for the improvements in girls' educational achievements over the last 40 years. [4]

_____

_____

_____

_____

_____

Perspectives on the Counter-School Culture

8 Identify and explain **one** way in which membership of a counter-school culture could influence students' educational achievements. [4]

An Introduction to Crime and Deviance

You must be able to:

- Explain the terms crime and deviance
- Explain the view that deviance is socially defined
- Describe how social order is maintained over time
- Explain the difference between formal and informal social control.

Defining Crime and Deviance

- **Crime** involves illegal actions such as robbery, **identity theft** and acts related to **terrorism** that break the criminal **law**. If detected, they can result in criminal proceedings.
- **Deviance** refers to behaviour such as eavesdropping that does not conform to a society's norms. It is disapproved of by most people and, if detected, can result in negative sanctions.
- Deviant behaviour includes both legal and illegal activities.
- Some illegal acts (such as using a hand-held phone when driving) are not necessarily considered deviant by everyone.

Deviance as Socially Defined Behaviour

- Many sociologists argue that crime involves legally defined behaviour while deviance involves **socially defined behaviour**.
- Whether or not an act is seen as deviant depends on who carries out the act and how other people react to it; how they see, define and label the act.
- What is classified as deviant also varies between cultures and changes over time.

Social Order

- Sociologists explore how **social order** is maintained over time. There are two main approaches to explaining social order: the consensus and conflict approaches.

Functionalism argues that modern society is based on value consensus or broad agreement among people regarding norms and values. This consensus arises from the socialisation process during which people learn society's norms and values. Social order is maintained over time because most people support, and agree to conform to, the rules.

The Marxist approach sees capitalist society as based on conflicting interests between two main social classes: the bourgeoisie and the proletariat. Class conflict occurs between them because they have opposing interests. Social order is maintained over time, however, because the bourgeoisie have the power to enforce order and influence the laws.

Key Point

Functionalism and Marxism are both structural approaches. This means that they focus on the structure of society and how it influences people. However, they disagree on how society is structured and how social order is maintained over time.

Formal Social Control

- Formal **social control** is based on laws and written rules and is linked to the ways in which the state controls people's behaviour.
- The **agencies of formal social control** are the bodies that make the laws, enforce them or punish law breakers.
  - The Houses of Parliament are the **legislature** and they make the laws that regulate behaviour.
  - The police maintain order, enforce the law, investigate crime and apprehend offenders.
  - The **judiciary** deal with alleged offenders and sentence those found guilty of crimes. **Magistrates** hear cases in the Magistrates' Court and deal with most criminal offences including minor assaults and theft. The Crown Court tries serious **indictable offences** before a judge and jury. If a person disagrees with a guilty verdict or a sentence, they may be granted the **right of appeal**.
  - The **prison service** keeps convicted offenders, who have received a prison sentence, in custody. Prisons punish and rehabilitate convicted lawbreakers, and deter them and others from committing crime.
  - The **probation service** supervises offenders who have been released into the community.

One purpose of prisons is to punish convicted lawbreakers.

Informal Social Control

- Informal social control is based on **unwritten rules** and processes, such as the approval or disapproval of other people. It is enforced via social pressure – by the reactions of **agencies of informal social control** such as family members, friends or colleagues.
- These reactions may take the form of positive or negative sanctions.
  - Positive sanctions reward individuals who comply with the group's expectations by, for example, praising them.
  - Negative sanctions punish those who do not conform by, for instance, ridiculing or ignoring them.

Informal social control operates in families.

Quick Test

1. Identify one similarity between crime and deviance.
2. Identify one difference between the functionalist and Marxist approaches to social order.
3. Identify one difference between formal and informal social control.

Key Words

crime	legislature
identity theft	judiciary
terrorism	magistrates
law	indictable offences
deviance	right to appeal
socially defined behaviour	prison service
social order	probation service
social control	unwritten rules
agencies of formal social control	agencies of informal social control

Functionalist and Interactionist Perspectives on Crime and Deviance

You must be able to:

- Describe and criticise Merton's functionalist perspective on crime and deviance
- Describe and criticise Becker's interactionist approach.

Merton's Functionalist Perspective and Anomie

- Merton (1938) argued that people's aspirations and goals are largely determined by the values of their culture. In the USA, for example, people are socialised to believe in the American Dream – the idea that anyone who works hard can become successful and rich, regardless of their background.
- Some people accept the goal of achieving economic success but lack opportunities to succeed through socially acceptable routes. Most working-class people, for example, have limited opportunities to find high-flying jobs with huge salaries.
- People may experience strain between the goals they have been socialised to strive for and the means of achieving them. In this situation, a condition of **anomie** (the breakdown of norms) develops. In other words, the norms that regulate behaviour break down and people turn to whatever means work for them to achieve material success. When anomie develops, high rates of crime (such as theft or fraud) and **delinquency** are likely.

Criticisms of Merton

- Juvenile delinquency such as vandalism is not motivated by the goal of making money.
- It is not clear why some individuals faced with anomie break the rules, while others conform.
- Many sociologists argue that society is based on conflict between powerful and subordinate groups rather than on consensus or shared values and goals.
- Marxists argue that Merton fails to consider power relations in society, or who makes the laws and benefits from them.

Key Thinker

Merton (1938)

Key Point

Merton (1938) explains crime and deviance in terms of the structure and culture of society. In other words, he puts forward a **structural theory** rather than focusing on an individual's genes or personality.

Acts of vandalism are not linked to the goal of achieving economic or material success.

Becker's Interactionist Perspective

- Interactionism explores the interaction between the person who commits an act and those who react to it.
- Becker (1963) argues that deviance is created by society. Social groups create deviance by making rules, applying these rules to particular people and labelling them as 'outsiders'.
- Whether or not a particular act is seen as deviant depends on how others react to it. This varies according to when and where the act takes place, who commits the act and who feels harmed by it.
- Some groups have the power to make rules and apply them to others. Power is related to age, gender, ethnicity and class. For instance, adults make many important rules for young people, such as those regarding school attendance.
- Becker explores how people develop **deviant careers** over time.
  - For example, a young woman uses illegal drugs, is caught and labelled a deviant. This label changes how others see her – she is now 'the local junkie'.
  - This new status becomes a **master status** and overrides her status as a daughter or employee. Her parents reject her; she loses her home, her friends and her job.
  - She resorts to criminal and deviant activities such as shoplifting to support her habit.
  - Finally, she moves into a group with a deviant sub-culture. The young woman now identifies with this deviant group and sees herself as one of them.
- Becker argues that labelling may produce a self-fulfilling prophecy – the person labelled may come to fit the image people have of them.

Criticisms of Becker and the Interactionist Approach
- Interactionism does not explain why individuals deviate in the first place.
- Interactionism sees criminals as victims of labelling rather than as people who choose to commit crime.
- Structural approaches argue that interactionism overlooks the influence of the social structure on behaviour. Marxists, for example, argue that interactionism does not focus enough on power inequalities between social classes.

Key Thinker

Becker (1963)

The concept of the self-fulfilling prophecy is also relevant to education.

Key Point

Merton (1938) and Becker (1963) are key thinkers, so it is important that you are familiar with their work on crime and deviance.

Quick Test
1. Sociologists explain involvement in crime and deviance in terms of social rather than biological or psychological factors. True or false?
2. According to Merton, what influences people's goals and aspirations?
3. According to Becker, who or what creates deviance?

Key Words

anomie
delinquency
structural theory
deviant careers
master status

Marxist and Feminist Explanations of Crime and Deviance

You must be able to:

- Explain Marxist theories of crime and deviance
- Explain feminist theories of crime and deviance
- Describe Heidensohn's key ideas on female conformity.

Marxist Approaches to Crime and Deviance

- Capitalist society is based on values such as materialism (valuing material possessions), consumerism (wanting the latest consumer goods such as mobile phones) and competition between individuals to obtain these products.
- In an unequal society, not everyone can afford the products of capitalism. Some people will try to get material goods through any means possible, including illegal means. Crime is a by-product of the way capitalist society is organised and the inequalities built into it.

Capitalism is based on materialism and consumerism.

Marxist Views on Law Enforcement

- Marxists are critical of the laws in a capitalist society. Criminal law is made by, and in the interests of, the bourgeoisie and many laws protect private property.
- **Agencies of social control** such as the police and courts operate in the interests of the powerful bourgeoisie and against the proletariat.
- Certain types of crime are likely to be targeted – street crime, for example, rather than **white-collar crime**.
- Certain groups such as black people and working-class people are more likely to be targeted, while crimes committed by the bourgeoisie may often go undetected or unpunished.

Criticisms of Marxist Approaches

- Not every criminal law supports the interests of the dominant class.
- Functionalists argue that society is based on value consensus rather than on conflict.
- Some feminists argue that Marxist approaches ignore issues of gender in patriarchal society.

> ### Key Point
>
> Marxist and functionalist approaches are both structural theories that explain crime and deviance in terms of the way society (the social structure) influences human behaviour. Marxists explain crime by examining the structure of capitalist society and who has power within it.

Feminist Perspectives on Crime and Deviance

- Feminist sociologists examine how female offenders are treated within the **criminal justice system** (CJS), including the police and the courts.
- The **double deviance thesis** suggests that the CJS treats some women more harshly than others. Female offenders (particularly those who deviate from gender **stereotypes**) are treated as double deviants because they have broken the norms governing gender behaviour as well as the law.
- Feminist perspectives examine the ways women are victimised in society. They question why domestic violence and sex crimes are under-reported to the police.

Heidensohn on Female Conformity

- Women have a lower rate of officially recorded crime than men and commit fewer serious crimes. Heidensohn (1985) uses **control theory** to explain this from a feminist perspective.
- Control theory emphasises the social bonds between people (for example, bonds between families and friends). Social bonds can prevent people from turning to crime and act as an agency of social control.
- Patriarchal society has separate spheres for men and women. Public life is seen as men's sphere and the home is seen as a woman's place.
- When studying female **criminality**, Heidensohn examines female **conformity** and the control of women. Patriarchal society controls women more effectively than men so it is harder for them to break the law. Women are controlled at home, in public and at work.
- Domestic life and marriage control women to ensure that they conform. Women's opportunities to commit crime are limited by their housewife role. Their time is taken up with housework and monitoring others (such as their children) within the home. As a result, women's role as mothers can constrain their behaviour.
- Women's behaviour in public is controlled by the fear of male violence. This fear controls their behaviour, for example by preventing them from going out after dark.
- In the workplace men have power over women, for example as managers or supervisors. Sexual harassment is a form of male control and limits women's freedom in the workplace.

Key Thinker

Heidensohn (1985)

Key Point

Heidensohn (1985) is a key thinker and, in her book, she draws on data from her study of delinquent girls. She also draws on a range of secondary sources, including **official crime statistics**, autobiographies, biographies and studies by other sociologists.

Think about the connections between Heidensohn's ideas on domestic life and marriage, and the topics of families and socialisation.

Key Words

agencies of social control
white-collar crime
criminal justice system
double deviance thesis
stereotypes
control theory
criminality
conformity
official crime statistics

Quick Test

1. Identify one similarity between Marxist and functionalist approaches to crime and deviance.
2. Identify one similarity between Marxist and feminist approaches to crime and deviance.

Statistical Data on the Extent of Crime

You must be able to:

- Describe the problems with official statistics of crimes recorded by the police
- Outline the different sociological perspectives on official crime statistics
- Describe victim surveys and self-report studies.

Sources of Statistical Data on Crime

The two main measures of crime levels are:

1. official statistics of crimes recorded by the police
2. surveys such as **victim surveys** and **self-report studies**.

Police-Recorded Crime

Problems with Police-Recorded Crime Statistics

- Official statistics of police-recorded crime provide an inaccurate picture of the total amount of crime committed.
  - Undiscovered crimes cannot be included.
  - Unreported crime cannot be recorded. Victims might see a crime as too trivial, or feel too embarrassed or scared to report it.
  - When crime is discovered in the workplace, employers may dismiss employees rather than involve the police.
  - The police do not record all **reported crime**. They may see a reported crime as too trivial to record (for example, petty vandalism) or doubt the report's accuracy.

Trends in Police-Recorded Crime

- Police-recorded crime statistics allow researchers to compare the **crime rate** in different areas and to identify trends over time.
- Statistics indicate that the overall volume of crime in England and Wales has been falling. However, the statistics may not provide an accurate measurement of crime rates or trends. If the levels of particular crimes such as violent incidents vary over time, this may reflect changes in spending on CCTV **surveillance**.
- The trends can be affected by changes in the way the police record crimes. For example, the rules about recording crime were changed in 1998 and in 2003, so it is difficult to compare over time.

> **Key Point**
>
> Official statistics of crimes recorded by the police appear to give a factual measure of the extent of crime in any one year. However, they ignore the **dark figure of crime**, which includes unreported and unrecorded crime.

> **Key Point**
>
> Official statistics on crime are a secondary source of quantitative data. The material here is relevant to research methods.

Perspectives on Police-Recorded Crime Statistics

Perspective	View on Police-Recorded Crime Statistics
Interpretivism	Crime statistics are a social construct. They are the outcome of various decisions made by victims, witnesses and police. They do not provide a true picture of crime levels.
Labelling theory	Behaviour only becomes deviant when people such as police officers define it as such. Crime statistics reflect police officers' power to define and label behaviour as criminal.
Marxism	The statistics reflect the class-based nature of capitalist society. White-collar and **corporate crime** are not policed effectively and are under-represented in the statistics.
Feminism	The statistics under-record incidents of violence against women, including domestic violence.

Victim Surveys

- Victim surveys ask people about their experiences of crime. The annual Crime Survey for England and Wales (CSEW), for example, is run by the Office for National Statistics. It measures crime through surveys with large samples of households.
- The CSEW interviews respondents about whether they have experienced particular crimes during the last 12 months, and, if so, which crimes and whether they reported them to the police.

Advantages of the CSEW	Disadvantages of the CSEW
Provides data on offences that are not counted in police-**recorded crime** statistics.	Does not cover all police-recorded crimes. For example, it excludes: • murder (where the victim is dead) • so-called victimless crimes (such as possession of drugs).
Trends in particular crimes (such as domestic burglary) can be identified.	Respondents may forget trivial crimes or lie about having reported crimes to the police. In this case, the findings will not be valid.
The results help policy makers to devise policies to tackle crime.	It is a household survey and does not question homeless people or people living in communal establishments such as prisons, student halls of residence or care homes.

Self-report Studies

- Self-report studies ask people about their offending. The Offending, Crime and Justice Survey (OCJS), for example, was commissioned by the Home Office and carried out annually between 2003 and 2006. It measured the extent of self-reported offending, drug use and **anti-social behaviour** in England and Wales, particularly among those aged 10 to 15 years.
- The OCJS provided data on some offenders and offences that were not dealt with by the police or courts. However, it only interviewed people living in households.

Self-report studies provide information on offenders and offences that the police or courts have not necessarily dealt with.

Quick Test

1. Identify one disadvantage of police-recorded crime statistics.
2. Self-report studies question respondents about their experiences as crime victims. True or false?

Factors Affecting Criminal and Deviant Behaviour

You must be able to:

- Explain the relationship between social class and crime
- Explain young people's involvement in criminal and deviant behaviour.

Social Class and Crime

- Official crime statistics indicate a relationship between people's involvement in crime and their social class, age, gender and ethnicity. Working-class people are over-represented in prisons.
- From a functionalist perspective, Merton uses anomie theory to explain crime (see page 74). In his view, everyone shares the American Dream of becoming rich and successful, regardless of their background. Crime results from unequal opportunities in society to get rich via legal means. When legal avenues are closed to working-class people, some may turn to crime to get rich.
- The statistics may reflect bias within the criminal justice system. Marxists argue that the agencies of social control target certain groups (such as working-class people) and certain crimes (such as street crime). By contrast, crimes such as business fraud committed by powerful groups are under-recorded.

White-collar Crime

- White-collar crime refers to crimes committed by people in relatively high-status positions (such as accountants or lawyers) during the course of their work. Examples include tax evasion and fraud.
- These crimes occur within the workplace so discovery can be difficult. Also, the police are often not called upon when an offence has been committed. So, much white-collar crime is likely to be undiscovered, unreported and unrecorded.

Corporate Crime

- Corporate crime refers to crimes committed by employees on behalf of the organisation they work for. It includes offences against consumers (such as the sale of unfit foods) and environmental offences (such as the pollution of rivers).
- It can be difficult to prosecute the crimes of big corporations, because they can afford skilled lawyers to fight their court cases.

Young People, Crime and Inadequate Socialisation

One environmental offence is the pollution of rivers.

- Official statistics indicate that criminal activity is more commonly found in particular social groups such as young males.

- Functionalist theories stress the importance of primary socialisation within families. If children are inadequately socialised into society's norms and values, they may engage in crime and deviance. Other agencies of socialisation, such as schools and religions, are also seen as failing to socialise children adequately.

Albert Cohen, Sub-cultural Theory and Delinquent Sub-cultures

- Sub-cultural theory explains juvenile delinquency and adult crime in terms of the values of a particular **sub-culture**. Albert Cohen (1955) studied juvenile delinquency among working-class boys in the USA.
- Cohen argued that juvenile delinquency is carried out by groups rather than individuals. Young males learn to become delinquents by joining gangs in which delinquent behaviour is 'the done thing'. Delinquency involves being part of a delinquent sub-culture among boys' gangs in **urban** neighbourhoods of large cities.
- Cohen linked juvenile delinquency to the education system. He argued that schools are based on middle-class values and expectations. Working-class boys cannot compete on equal terms with middle-class boys to get status and qualifications through education.
- Working-class boys experience **status frustration** in trying but failing to meet middle-class expectations at school. Being part of a delinquent sub-culture enables these boys to gain status within their group and hit back at a school system that has branded them as failures.

Being part of a delinquent subculture can bring status.

Criticisms of Albert Cohen

- Cohen's work shows a middle-class bias. He assumes that working-class delinquents start out by accepting middle-class aspirations such as educational success.
- Cohen focuses on delinquent boys in gangs. Feminists question how far his explanation applies to girls.

Key Thinker

Albert Cohen (1955)

Deviancy has been linked to school sub-cultures in Britain. From a Marxist perspective, Paul Willis (1977) focuses on the 'lads' in a secondary school in the Midlands and their anti-school culture.

Key Point

Albert Cohen's sub-cultural theory links delinquency to a range of factors including social class, gender and age.

Key Point

Albert Cohen (1955) is a key thinker, so it is important that you are familiar with his ideas on sub-cultural theory and delinquent sub-cultures.

Quick Test

1. Offences against consumers and environmental offences are examples of white-collar crime. True or false?
2. Identify one criticism of Albert Cohen's ideas from a feminist perspective.
3. Merton links crime among working-class people to their aspiration to become rich. What does Cohen link delinquency among working-class boys to?

Key Words

sub-culture
urban
status frustration

Other Factors Affecting Criminal and Deviant Behaviour

You must be able to:

- Describe and explain the relationship between gender and crime
- Describe the ideas of Pat Carlen on female offenders
- Describe and explain the relationship between ethnicity and crime.

Gender and Crime: Lesser Involvement

- Official statistics suggest that females are less likely to offend (and reoffend) than males and less likely to commit indictable offences.

Remember to look out for links or connections between the different topics. For example, the concept of socialisation is also relevant to families and education.

Explanations for Women's Lesser Involvement in Crime

Explanation	Reason
Gender socialisation	In general, girls are socialised to be more passive and boys more active. This may lead males into criminal activity.
Different opportunities	Females have fewer opportunities than males to commit crimes because their behaviour is more closely controlled and they often have more domestic responsibilities than men.
The **chivalry thesis**	Female offenders may be treated more leniently than males because professionals within the criminal justice system (CJS) hold stereotyped beliefs about gender. For example, female offenders are seen as needing help rather than punishment.

Women often have more caring responsibilities than men and fewer opportunities to commit crime.

The Increasing Involvement of Women in Crime

- The number of female offenders aged 21 years and over is increasing in the UK, and more women are being arrested for violence.
- Explanations for this include the following:
  - The changing position of women in society: women have lost many of the controls that deterred them from crime. They now have similar legal and illegal opportunities to men.
  - The rise in ladette-type behaviour among some young women related, for example, to drinking and fighting. This has been linked to young women's increased confidence and assertiveness.
  - More women are now being arrested, charged and convicted: changing attitudes towards female criminality mean that women are no longer treated more leniently within the CJS.
  - **Poverty**: women are more likely than men to work in low paid jobs. Women's increased involvement in crime is linked to their economic situation.

The issue of poverty is also relevant to education and social stratification.

Carlen on Women, Crime and Poverty

- Carlen (1988) focuses on gender, social class and crime from a feminist perspective.
- She argues that working-class women are expected to make the **class deal** and the **gender deal**.
  - The class deal offers them material rewards such as consumer goods if they work for a wage.
  - The gender deal offers material and emotional rewards if they live with a male breadwinner within the family.
- When these rewards are not available or turn out not to be worth it, the class and gender deals break down. At this point, crime becomes a possibility.
- The women in Carlen's study identified four major factors linked to their law breaking:
  - poverty
  - living in residential care
  - drug addiction
  - the search for excitement.
- Poverty and being in care led them to reject the class and gender deals.
- Most of the women lacked legitimate ways of earning a decent living. They had little experience of the rewards of the class deal, such as consumer goods. Crime was a way of trying to solve the problems of poverty.
- Having lived in residential care, many of the women had not experienced the rewards of the gender deal such as fulfilment from family life. They had nothing to lose by committing crime.

Ethnicity and Crime

- Statistics show that members of some ethnic groups are over-represented in prisons. Black people are much more likely than white people to be stopped and searched by the police.
- Crime among some members of minority ethnic groups has been linked to unemployment, poverty and deprivation.
- The statistics may reflect the way policing is carried out and bias within the CJS. Black people are more likely to be targeted, prosecuted, convicted and sentenced for longer periods than people from other ethnic groups.
- Other explanations focus on **racial discrimination** and institutional racism within the police and other parts of the CJS.

 Key Thinker

Carlen (1988)

 Key Point

Pat Carlen (1988) is a key thinker. It is important that you are familiar with her work on gender and crime, including her research methods. In the study discussed here, she conducted unstructured interviews with 39 female offenders aged 15 to 46 years, most of whom were working class.

 Key Point

Carlen draws on control theory (see page 77), which argues that people are controlled through a 'deal' that offers them rewards for conforming. She argues that working-class women are controlled through the class deal and the gender deal.

 Key Words

chivalry thesis
poverty
class deal
gender deal
racial discrimination

 Quick Test

1. Identify one way in which females are controlled in society.
2. Identify one reason why members of some ethnic groups are over-represented in prisons.

The Media and Public Debates over Crime

You must be able to:

- Explain the media's role in the amplification of deviance
- Identify and describe some of the public debates about criminal and deviant behaviour.

The Role of the Media in the Amplification of Deviance

- Stan Cohen (1972) argues that the media help to create moral panics. A moral panic involves exaggerating the extent and significance of a social problem. A particular group is cast as a **folk devil**, defined as a threat to society's values and portrayed in stereotyped ways by the media.
- Stan Cohen undertook a case study of the moral panic surrounding skirmishes between mods and rockers in Clacton, an English coastal resort, in 1964. The incidents were reported in most national newspapers with sensationalist headlines. In this way, the mods and rockers were cast as folk devils.
- The media exaggerated the seriousness of the events in terms of the numbers of young people taking part, the numbers involved in violence and the amount of damage.
- The media created a false **image** of young people and their activities. Cohen describes this as **deviancy amplification** – exaggerating and distorting the events that happened. This amplification encouraged other young people to behave in ways portrayed by the media, resulting in further disturbances and a public outcry or moral panic.
- People reading newspapers and watching scenes on television began to see the mods and rockers as a threat to law and order. The police, responding to the public outcry, acted harshly which led to further arrests. Cohen argues that the media can actually amplify deviance or provoke more of it.

> ### Key Point
>
> Recent moral panics have surrounded school violence, bullying, school shootouts, **benefit cheats**, single mothers, refugees and **asylum seekers**.

Public Debates over Criminal and Deviant Behaviour

Media Coverage of Crime

- The media play a role in **agenda setting** by focusing on some items and views, and excluding others. So the public come to see particular issues as social problems.
- The media operate with a set of values about what is considered 'newsworthy'. Media **gatekeepers** decide what to cover and how to present it. Editors allocate staff, space and time to topics according to their **news values**, and see crime as newsworthy.

- One view is that the media intensify public concerns about law and order. Research suggests that violent crimes are over-represented compared with their incidence in official crime statistics. The term **media amplification** describes the way the media exaggerate the importance of an issue by over-reporting it.

Concerns about Youth Crime

- Teenage knife crime is costly in terms of the young lives lost.
- Vandalism can be costly in economic terms.
- Anti-social behaviour (such as drunken behaviour or damaging bus shelters) is seen as a problem because it generates fear, which damages community life.
- **Youth crime** is considered newsworthy within the media. It is often front-page news in the UK and, as a result, is a source of public anxiety. Young people can become **scapegoats** who are blamed for society's problems.

Sentencing

- The lack of clarity about sentencing policy is an area of public concern. For example, some prisoners are released before the end of their prison term and people do not necessarily understand how this early release works.
- The prison regime and sentencing are seen as too soft. One view is that prison sentences do not punish prisoners effectively or repair the harm caused to crime victims.
- Another concern is whether particular groups (such as vulnerable people) who have not committed serious offences should be imprisoned at all.

The Prison System and the Treatment of Young Offenders

- Major issues facing prisons include overcrowding, cuts in prison staff numbers, and the levels of suicide and self-harm among prisoners.
- There is concern about how young offenders are treated within the criminal justice system. Some young adults have died in custody. Other concerns include the levels of suicide, self-harm and violence among young offenders in custody.

>
> ## Key Point
>
> Violent crime (including gun and knife crime) is another focus of public debate.

Alcohol-related violence is a focus of public debate.

> ## Key Words
>
> folk devil
> image
> deviancy amplification
> benefit cheats
> asylum seekers
> agenda setting
> gatekeepers
> news values
> media amplification
> youth crime
> scapegoats

> ## Quick Test
>
> 1. Identify three groups who have been the focus of a moral panic.
> 2. Describe what the term 'gatekeeper' means.
> 3. Describe what the term 'scapegoat' means.

The Role of Education from a Functionalist Perspective

1   Describe **one** example of achieved status.   [3]

The Marxist Approach to Education

2   Which term is used by sociologists to describe the things learnt in school (such as valuing obedience) that are not formally taught in lessons? Shade **one** box only.   [1]

A   Formal curriculum   ◯

B   National curriculum   ◯

C   Vocational curriculum   ◯

D   Hidden curriculum   ◯

Different Types of School

3 Describe **one** form of educational provision in Britain that is not funded by the state. [3]

....

....

....

....

....

....

....

Social Class and Educational Achievement

4 Describe one example of marketisation in schools. [3]

....

....

....

....

....

....

....

The Impact of School Processes on Working-Class Students' Achievements

5 Identify and describe **one** example of how labelling processes can affect students' achievements in schools. [3]

....

....

....

....

....

....

....

....

Ethnicity and Educational Achievement

6 Identify and describe **one** example of an ethnic group in Britain. [3]

....

....

....

....

....

....

....

....

Gender and Educational Achievement

7 Identify and explain **one** reason for the educational underachievement of boys. [4]

_____

_____

_____

_____

_____

_____

_____

_____

_____

_____

Perspectives on the Counter-School Culture

8 Identify and explain **one** disadvantage of using questionnaires to research counter-school cultures. [4]

_____

_____

_____

_____

_____

_____

Continue your answer on a separate piece of paper.

An Introduction to Crime and Deviance

1 Describe **one** example of deviance.   [3]

_____

_____

_____

_____

_____

_____

_____

Functionalist and Interactionist Perspectives on Crime and Deviance

2 Describe **one** example of a master status experienced by people who commit deviant acts.   [3]

_____

_____

_____

_____

_____

_____

_____

Marxist and Feminist Explanations of Crime and Deviance

3 Describe **one** example of a white-collar crime. [3]

Statistical Data on the Extent of Crime

4 Describe a victim survey. [3]

5 Which term is used by sociologists to describe unrecorded crime? Shade **one** box only.　　[1]

   A Dark figure of crime   ◯   **C** Self-reported crime   ◯

   B Victimless crime   ◯   **D** Crime rate   ◯

Factors Affecting Criminal and Deviant Behaviour

6 Identify and explain **one** reason why some young people commit crime.　　[4]

Other Factors Affecting Criminal and Deviant Behaviour

7 Describe the chivalry effect experienced by some women within the criminal justice system.　　[3]

The Media and Public Debates over Crime

8 Identify and explain **one** advantage of using unstructured interviews to investigate people's concerns about youth crime in the UK. [4]

An Introduction to Social Stratification

You must be able to:

- Explain the terms social stratification and social inequality
- Identify different types of stratification
- Describe and criticise Davis and Moore's functionalist theory of stratification.

Social Stratification and Social Inequality

- The term social stratification describes the way society is structured into a hierarchy of unequal strata or layers.
  - A social hierarchy is shaped like a pyramid and each layer is more powerful than the one below it.
  - The most privileged group forms the top layer and the least privileged group forms the bottom layer.
- Social inequality refers to the uneven distribution of resources (such as money and power) and opportunities related, for example, to education, employment and health.
- Stratification involves inequality between groups in the distribution of economic and social resources such as **wealth**, **income**, status and power. The group in the top rank of the hierarchy is likely to have much more wealth, income, status or power than those beneath.
- In the UK today, social class, gender, ethnicity and age are the main criteria by which people tend to be stratified.

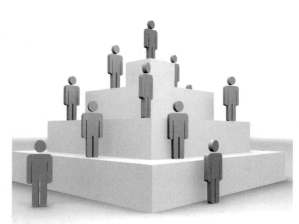

Different Forms of Stratification

- Stratification systems differ according to whether status (or social position) is ascribed (fixed at birth) or achieved (earned on the basis of merit).
- They also differ according to how open or closed they are. In an open system, social mobility is possible but in a closed system, it is unlikely.
- **Slavery** existed as a form of stratification in Ancient Greece and Rome, and in the southern states of the USA in the 19th century. Under slavery, one group claims the right to own another group and treats them as property.
- Other types of stratification include the **caste** system in traditional India, **feudalism** in medieval Europe, and the social class system in the UK today.

Davis and Moore: The Functionalist Theory of Stratification

- Davis and Moore (1945) argue that all societies need a way of placing individuals into the different roles or social positions that must be filled (known as role allocation).
- Some roles are functionally more important for society than others. For example, they provide essential services and ensure society's survival over time.
- Most people lack the talent to fill these **functionally important roles** or the motivation to train for them. To attract the most talented people, these roles must provide access to desirable rewards such as high pay and status.
- Stratification is functionally necessary for society because it ensures that the most talented people train for and fill the most important jobs.
- All societies must treat people differently in terms of their status and rewards. So all societies must have some degree of inequality built into them. This inequality is functional, however, because people accept it as fair.

One view is that society needs a system of unequal rewards to match highly talented and well-trained individuals to functionally important roles.

Criticisms of Davis and Moore
- Many jobs that are vital to society have relatively low pay (for example, nursing) or low status (for example, refuse collection).
- A group's high pay and status may be linked to its power rather than to the functional importance of its position.
- Davis and Moore assume that society is meritocratic but critics disagree.
- Rather than seeing stratification as functional, Marxists view it as a means by which a privileged minority exploit others. Neither inequality nor stratification is inevitable.
- Marxist and feminist perspectives see stratification as a system in which some groups in society (such as the bourgeoisie or men) gain at the expense of others.

 Key Thinkers

Davis and Moore (1945)

Look out for links between the functions of education (such as selection) and the functions of stratification.

Key Point

The American sociologists Davis and Moore (1945) are key thinkers, so it is important that you are familiar with their functionalist perspective on stratification.

Quick Test

1. Caste – in which status is ascribed – is an example of a stratification system linked to Hinduism in traditional India. True or false?
2. Social inequality refers to the division of society into a hierarchy of layers, with the most privileged at the top and the least privileged at the bottom. True or false?
3. Identify one function of social stratification.

 Key Words

wealth
income
slavery
caste
feudalism
functionally important
  roles

Different Views of Social Class

You must be able to:

- Describe Marx's key ideas on social class
- Describe Weber's key ideas on social class
- Explain social class as a type of stratification.

Karl Marx: Social Class in the 19th Century

- Karl Marx identified two main classes in capitalist society: the bourgeoisie and the proletariat.
- Class membership is determined by economic factors – by ownership and non-ownership of the means of production.
- The wealthy bourgeoisie own the means of production and the proletariat sell their labour to the bourgeoisie in order to survive.
- The proletariat experience **alienation** under capitalism because they lack control over production and the products of their labour.
- Other classes include the lumpenproletariat (such as the 'drop-outs' and criminals of society) and the petty bourgeoisie (such as the owners of small businesses).
- The two main classes have opposing interests. The bourgeoisie want ever-increasing profits and the proletariat seek higher wages. The bourgeoisie exploit the proletariat, leading to class struggle or conflict.
- The bourgeoisie's position is justified by **ruling-class ideology**; for example, ideas about competition and the free market disguise the reality of exploitation. This ruling-class ideology leads to **false class consciousness** among the proletariat, who, for example, are unaware of the true nature of social relationships under capitalism.
- Marx argued that, over time, the bourgeoisie would get smaller and much richer. The petty bourgeoisie, unable to compete, would sink into the proletariat. The proletariat would get bigger and increasingly poor. Eventually, the proletariat would rebel, leading to a revolution. Following this, the means of production would be communally owned, resulting in a classless society.

Weber: Social Class in the Late 19th and Early 20th Centuries

- Max Weber argued that classes are formed in the labour market, where one class of people hires labour and another class sells their labour. The processes of hiring labour and the rewards (or **life chances**) from this are crucial in explaining class.

 Key Thinkers

Marx (1818–1883) and Weber (1864–1920)

 Key Point

Marx and Weber are key thinkers, so it is important that you understand their ideas on social class.

- Weber argued that a class is a group of people who have similar life chances; that is, chances of being successful (or otherwise) in life and opportunities in education, health, and so on. Weber identified four main social classes: property owners, professionals, the petty bourgeoisie (for example, shopkeepers) and the working class.
- These different classes have different **market situations** or life chances in the labour market. Working-class people, for example, all share similar life chances in the labour market. However, they have different life chances from property owners.
- Like Marx, Weber saw class as based on the distribution of economic resources such as wealth. However, Weber also stressed the importance of non-economic factors such as status and power (political influence) in determining life chances.
- Status groups are identified by the prestige attached to their lifestyle. Each of the four classes had a different amount of status, wealth and power.
- A person's status may differ from their class (or economic) position. For instance, even though members of the **aristocracy** (such as a Lord or Lady) may not be wealthy property owners, their title gives them status.

Members of the Royal Family gain status from their titles.

Stratification Based on Social Class Today

- In Britain today, social class (or socio-economic class) is seen as the main form of stratification.
- Social class is based on economic factors such as occupation (how people earn a living). Occupation is used to measure class because it is linked to levels of pay, working conditions and status.
- **Subjective class** refers to how people see themselves in class terms.
- There are three social classes in Britain: the working, middle and **upper class**. Some **New Right** commentators argue that Britain also has an underclass (see pages 104–105).
- In class-based societies, gender, ethnicity and age are also sources of inequality.
  - For example, middle-class men and women may have different life chances in relation to pay and promotion at work.

Factors Affecting Life Chances

You must be able to:

- Explain factors affecting life chances including gender, ethnicity, age, disability, sexuality and religion.

Life Chances

- Life chances refer to people's chances of having positive or negative outcomes (such as being healthy or ill) over their lifetime in relation to, for example, their health, education, employment and housing.
- Life chances are distributed unequally between groups because they are affected by factors such as class position, gender and ethnicity.
  - For example, middle-class people (such as lawyers) have more chance of accessing good quality healthcare than working-class people.
- Life chances are shaped by inequalities in wealth, income, power and status.

Inequalities Based on Gender

- Feminists focus on gender inequalities in society. Over the last 50 years, anti-discrimination legislation (such as the Sex Discrimination Act 1975) has addressed aspects of gender inequality in education and employment.
- Despite this, feminist approaches argue that gender is still a key division in society. For example, the gender pay gap persists because women are more likely than men to work in low-paid and part-time jobs. Women are held back by a **glass ceiling** which acts as an invisible barrier to promotion. Some occupations are either male-dominated or female-dominated. For example, although the proportion of female fire fighters in England is increasing, it was only 3.9 per cent in 2010.
- Explanations for the persistence of gender inequalities at work include sex discrimination in the workplace, women's triple shift (combining paid work, domestic labour and emotion work) and inadequate childcare provision.
- Some feminist approaches argue that society is patriarchal in that men have power within families, politics and the workplace, and generally receive a bigger share of rewards such as income, wealth and status.

Inequalities Based on Ethnicity

- Over the last 50 years, laws (such as the Race Relations Act 1976) have addressed inequality based on ethnicity in areas including education, employment and criminal justice.
- Many employers have equal opportunities policies to support equality and diversity. Awareness of institutional racism has been raised within organisations such as the police service.

> ### Key Point
>
> Many sociologists see class, gender and ethnicity as interrelated rather than separate aspects of inequality. White, middle-class men may experience advantages based on class, gender and ethnicity, while black working-class women may experience disadvantages.

- Many sociologists argue, however, that little has changed in the fields of employment, education, politics and criminal justice.
  - For example, UK unemployment rates are higher among people of Asian and Black Caribbean heritage than among White people. Men and women of Pakistani and Bangladeshi heritage have much worse chances of getting professional and managerial jobs than their white peers of the same age and educational level.
- Explanations for the persistence of inequality at work include **racism** and discrimination in the labour market.
- Marxist approaches see racism (and sexism) as built into the workings of capitalism. Some groups (including people from minority ethnic groups and working-class women) are hired during economic booms and fired during recessions when capitalism no longer needs them.

Inequalities Based on Age

- Sociologists argue that age (like gender and ethnicity) is socially constructed and that expectations surrounding age vary historically and cross-culturally.
  - For example, child labour was the norm among working-class families in 19th-century Britain and exists in some parts of the world today.
- The term **ageism** (or age discrimination) describes a situation in which someone is treated differently and less favourably based on their age. For example, a person in their 60s may be denied promotion at work because their employer believes that they are too old to learn new skills.
- Young people and older people are more vulnerable to ageism and stereotyping than other groups.
- In Britain, there are now regulations against age discrimination in employment and training.
- The Equality Act 2010 protects people from age discrimination at work and when accessing services in places such as banks or hotels.
- The unemployment rate for young people aged 16 to 24 years is higher than for older groups.

Disability, Sexuality, Religion and Beliefs

- Despite legislation such as the Equality Act 2010, people's life chances can be influenced by disability, sexuality, and religion and beliefs, if they experience discrimination in education and the workplace.
- Some groups experience hate crime that is motivated by hostility or prejudice related to their religion, sexuality or disability.

Key Point

Marxist approaches see social class in capitalist societies as more significant than gender or ethnicity. Feminist approaches see gender inequalities in patriarchal societies as more significant.

Legislation now protects people from age discrimination.

 Quick Test

1. Identify one way in which governments have tried to tackle discrimination.
2. The glass ceiling refers to invisible walls between different occupations. True or false?

 Key Words

glass ceiling
racism
ageism

Studies of Affluent Workers

You must be able to:

- Describe the affluent worker study
- Describe Devine's work on revisiting the affluent worker
- Explain the term social mobility.

The Embourgeoisement Thesis

- In the late 1950s and early 1960s, some sociologists suggested that affluent working-class families were becoming middle class in their norms and values.
- According to this **embourgeoisement thesis**, their **affluence** led them to adopt privatised lifestyles centred on home and family, and to have aspirations based on consumerism.

The Affluent Worker Study

- Goldthorpe *et al.* (1969) tested the embourgeoisement thesis in the early 1960s. They interviewed affluent workers and their wives from three companies in Luton (including Vauxhall Motors) about their attitudes to work, lifestyles, aspirations and political views.
- Goldthorpe rejected the embourgeoisement thesis but argued that affluent workers may be part of a 'new' working class that resembled the middle class in terms of their privatised, home-centred lifestyles.
  - Affluent workers had an instrumental attitude to paid work – their work was a means to an end (a way of earning money to improve their living standards) rather than an end in itself (to get job satisfaction or make friends).
  - Affluent workers supported the Labour Party for individual gain and their attitude to trade unions was instrumental. Unlike the traditional working class, they were not motivated by working-class solidarity and the idea of 'sticking together'.

Fiona Devine: Affluent Workers Revisited

- Fiona Devine (1992) revisited Luton to explore how far working-class people's lifestyles were privatised (centred on the nuclear family within the home) in the 1980s.
- Devine compared her own findings with those of Goldthorpe's study. She argued that working-class lifestyles, norms and values have not changed as much as Goldthorpe suggested.
  - Her sample did not have purely privatised and home-centred lifestyles and social relationships.
  - The interviewees were not purely instrumental or motivated solely by the desire to improve their living standards.
  - Their aspirations and their social and political values were not solely individualistic. There was plenty of evidence of solidarity among the interviewees rather than individualism.

Key Point

A **privatised nuclear family** is cut off from the extended family – the lifestyle focuses on the home. **Privatised instrumentalism** refers to social relationships centred on the home. There is an instrumental attitude to work – it is a means to an end, rather than an end in itself.

Key Thinker

Fiona Devine (1992)

Key Point

Devine carried out intensive interviews with 62 Luton residents when she revisited Luton between 1986 and 1987. The men worked in shop-floor jobs at the Vauxhall car factory and some of the women also worked there.

Think about how Devine's work links to families.

Social Mobility

- The term 'social mobility' refers to people's movement up or down a society's strata, for example between social classes.
  - **Inter-generational** social mobility refers to movement between the generations of a family and occurs when a child enters a different class from their parents.
  - **Intra-generational** social mobility refers to the movement of an individual between social classes over their lifetime as a result, for example, of promotion.
- Routes to upward mobility include educational credentials and marriage. Changes in the occupational structure (such as a growth in white-collar work) may increase the chances of upward mobility. Barriers to upward social mobility include discrimination based on ethnicity or gender, and lack of skills and educational credentials.

Social Mobility in the UK

- Research indicates that children from working-class backgrounds have less chance of moving into professional occupations than children from professional backgrounds. Evidence suggests that social mobility fell towards the end of the 20th century in the UK. Children born into manual working-class families in 1958 had a better chance of moving into higher occupations than children born into similar families in the 1970s.
- This decrease in mobility is partly due to changes in the occupational structure. Skilled manual jobs have declined and the growth in professional jobs has slowed down.
- Statistical evidence from 2005 suggests that the UK has lower rates of social mobility than countries such as Canada, Norway and Denmark.
- Sociologists know more about what has happened to social mobility in the past than what is happening today. This is because an individual's outcome or destination cannot be known until they reach middle age.

Problems in Measuring Social Mobility

- Some studies of inter-generational mobility focus on males and reveal nothing about women's mobility.
- Research participants may not remember their employment histories, or those of their parents.
- There are problems in deciding which point in a person's career to measure mobility from.

> **Key Point**
>
> Social mobility is an important measure of how open society is. High rates of mobility suggest that status is achieved and society is meritocratic.

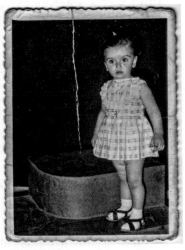

Working-class children born in the late 1950s in the UK had better chances of upward social mobility than those born in the 1970s.

> **Key Words**
>
> embourgeoisement thesis
> affluence
> privatised nuclear family
> privatised instrumentalism
> inter-generational

> **Quick Test**
>
> 1. A privatised nuclear family's lifestyle and social relationships focus on the home and the immediate family. True or false?
> 2. Privatised instrumentalism refers to social relationships centred on the home rather than work. Paid work is a means to an end. True or false?

Wealth, Income and Poverty

You must be able to:

- Explain the terms wealth, income and poverty
- Outline different ways of defining and measuring poverty
- Describe Townsend's work on relative deprivation
- Describe some groups who are at risk of poverty.

Wealth and Income

- Stratification involves the unequal distribution of resources such as wealth and income. Wealth refers to the ownership of assets such as houses and land as well as savings and shares. It is often inherited within families.
- Income refers to the flow of resources that individuals and households receive over a specific period of time. People receive income in cash (for example, wages) or in kind (for example, petrol allowances).

Defining Poverty

- There are two broad approaches to defining poverty – the absolute and relative approaches.
  - People experience **absolute poverty** when their income is insufficient to obtain the minimum needed to survive.
  - People experience **relative poverty** when their income is well below average, so they are poor compared with others in their society.
- Poverty can involve **social exclusion** when people are shut out from everyday activities and customs. In this case, poverty is not just about low incomes. It is also about excluding people from activities that most people take for granted.
- The definition of poverty adopted by the state is important because it determines how far government accepts that poverty exists and the policies to address it.

Measuring Poverty

- There are several different measures of poverty. The main official UK government measure is in terms of low incomes. Low incomes are those below 60 per cent of the median (middle point) income of the population after housing costs.
  - **Subjective poverty** is based on whether people see themselves as living in poverty.
  - **Environmental poverty** measures deprivation in terms of conditions such as inadequate housing and air pollution.

Townsend: Poverty in the UK

- Peter Townsend (1979) aimed to discover how many people were living in poverty in the UK.

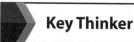

Key Thinker

Townsend (1979)

- He developed a deprivation index to measure **relative deprivation**.
- His index listed 12 items such as 'Household does not usually have a Sunday joint (3 in 4 times)'.
- Townsend found that almost 23 per cent of the UK population were in poverty. This proportion was much higher than that based on the **state standard of poverty** (at 6.1 per cent) and the **relative income standard of poverty** (at nine per cent).

Criticism of Townsend's Deprivation Index

- Critics question some of the items in Townsend's index (for example, a Sunday joint) and how they were selected. Not eating meat regularly is not necessarily linked to deprivation.
- If the index is inadequate, then the statistics based on it will also be questioned.

Groups at Risk of Poverty

- The chances of experiencing poverty are distributed unequally.

Ethnicity and Poverty

- People in UK households headed by someone from a minority ethnic group (particularly Pakistani or Bangladeshi heritage) are at risk of living in low-income households.
- Minority ethnic groups, for example, are generally disadvantaged in terms of unemployment, pay and the quality of their jobs.
- Explanations for this include racism and discrimination in the labour market.

Gender and Poverty

- Women are more at risk of poverty than men. There are several reasons for this.
  - Women have longer life expectancies than men but are less likely to have an occupational pension.
  - Women are more likely than men to head lone-parent families with low incomes.
  - The gender pay gap: many female-dominated jobs (for example, in sales and customer service) are relatively poorly paid.
  - Women are more likely than men to work in part-time employment.

Child Poverty

- Children are particularly vulnerable to poverty if they live in a family with four or more children, or where the head of household is a lone parent, from a minority ethnic group or workless.
- Poverty has a negative impact on children's life chances including their life expectancy, health, housing, educational attainments and job prospects.

Not eating meat may be linked to religious beliefs or vegetarianism rather than to deprivation.

> **Key Point**
>
> Townsend used a face-to-face survey of UK households in his landmark study of poverty. He was a pioneer in the study of poverty because he focused on deprivation and viewed it in relative terms.

> **Key Point**
>
> Poverty is linked to age, with children and pensioners more at risk of poverty than other age groups. People with disabilities are also more at risk of poverty.

> **Key Words**
>
> absolute poverty
> relative poverty
> social exclusion
> subjective poverty
> environmental poverty
> relative deprivation
> state standard of poverty
> relative income standard
> of poverty

> **Quick Test**
>
> 1. Identify one way of measuring poverty.
> 2. Identify one criticism of Townsend's deprivation index.

Different Explanations of Poverty

You must be able to:

- Outline the culture of poverty and the cycle of deprivation
- Describe and criticise Murray's key ideas on the underclass, including links to New Right theories
- Describe functionalist, Marxist and feminist perspectives on poverty
- Outline other approaches to poverty.

The Culture of Poverty and Cycle of Deprivation

- People from the poorest section of society are socialised within a sub-culture of poverty. They develop a way of life and a set of values to cope with their situation. For instance, they live for the moment (immediate gratification) and see no point in planning ahead.
- However, these values discourage them from staying on at school or saving money for the future and, in this way, escaping poverty.
- Poverty involves both material and cultural deprivation. It persists from one generation to the next, locking families into a **cycle of deprivation**.
- Critics argue that while this explanation may describe how poverty persists between generations, it fails to explain why some groups fall into poverty in the first place.

Murray and New Right Explanations

- Murray (1984) examined US governments' social policies since the late 1960s that aimed to reduce poverty. He focused on the impact of these policies on the behaviour of members of the underclass.
- In his view, the policies actually produced poverty and encouraged more people to become dependent on **welfare benefits**.
  - For example, they led to an increase in unmarried young mothers and encouraged a hard core of unemployed young people to have no interest in finding jobs and to become welfare dependent.
- Murray associated the underclass with poor African-American and Hispanic people. He argues that the underclass is growing and poses a threat to society's well-being because its members are responsible for increases in crime rates and are a burden to taxpayers.

The Underclass in the UK
- Murray (1996) argued that the UK's underclass is growing rapidly.
- He focused on the behaviour of the 'undeserving poor' and examined three measures of the underclass:
  - rising crime rates
  - an increase in the number of 'illegitimate' births
  - drop-out from the labour force among working-age men.
- He argued that **welfare reform** encouraged crime, single parenthood and unemployment, and took away the incentive to work.

 Key Point

Many sociologists argue that explanations of poverty should focus on the way society is structured rather than the behaviour of individuals or families.

 Key Thinker

Charles Murray (1984)

 Key Point

The American political scientist Charles Murray (1984) focuses on the underclass from a New Right approach. He draws on official statistics including unemployment, crime and extra-marital birth rates.

Criticisms of the New Right Approach

- Critics reject the idea that an underclass with different attitudes actually exists.
- The term is used to 'blame the victims' for their misfortunes.
- The underclass are used as a scapegoat for the problems in society.
- When explaining poverty, sociologists should focus on the structure of society and the 'overclass' – the rich and powerful groups in society.

Sociological Perspectives on Poverty

Functionalism and Poverty

- Poverty performs positive functions for some groups in society; e.g. it helps ensure that dirty and dangerous work gets done cheaply.
- Critics argue that functionalism tries to defend the existence of poverty rather than explain it.

Marxism and Poverty

- Poverty is the inevitable outcome of the class-based divisions in capitalist society. Capitalism generates extreme wealth for the bourgeoisie and poverty within the proletariat.
- Poverty serves the bourgeoisie's interests as they can hire and fire workers as needed. The fear of poverty and unemployment can be used to discipline the workers, keeping wages down and profits up.

Capitalism generates extreme wealth for the bourgeoisie.

Feminism and Poverty

- Women (particularly lone mothers and older widows) face a greater risk of poverty than men. Possible reasons include the gender pay gap and inequality in the division of caring responsibilities. Women are also more likely to outlive their partners.

Other Approaches to Poverty

- During economic recessions, unemployment levels rise and poverty increases.
- Welfare benefits are too low and the value of benefits and state pensions should be increased.

The Impact of Globalisation on UK Poverty

- The downturn in the global economy led to a financial crisis and recession in the UK between 2008 and 2010. This resulted in increased job insecurity and unemployment.
- Rising global fuel and food costs led to increases in the costs of living, which particularly affects people on low incomes.
- Some commentators argue that **globalisation** has increased inequality within the UK.

> ### Key Point
>
> Individual accounts of poverty (such as the cycle of deprivation and New Right) examine the behaviour or lifestyles of individuals and groups in poverty. Structural accounts (such as Marxism) examine how economic, social and political structures generate poverty.

> ### Key Words
>
> cycle of deprivation
> welfare benefits
> welfare reform
> globalisation

Quick Test

1. Identify one individual account of poverty.
2. Which approach is Charles Murray associated with?

Power and Authority

You must be able to:

- Describe the key ideas of Weber on power and authority
- Outline Marxist and feminist approaches to power
- Describe the key ideas of Walby on patriarchy
- Outline power relationships in everyday situations.

Weber on Power and Authority

- Max Weber (1947) argued that an individual or group exercises power when they get what they want, despite any opposition.
- Power is based on either coercion or **authority**.
  - Coercion involves the threat or use of force including physical violence. People obey because they feel they have no choice – they are forced into obeying against their will.
  - Authority is exercised over people when they willingly agree to obey an individual or group because they see it as the right thing to do. Force is unnecessary because people consent to power being exercised over them.
- Weber identified three types of authority: **traditional authority**, **rational legal authority** and **charismatic authority**. In each case, the people who are subjected to authority (such as students in classrooms) accept the exercise of power (in this case by the teacher) as legitimate.
  - Traditional authority is based on custom and tradition. In the UK, for example, the authority of the **monarchy** is based on tradition.
  - Rational legal authority is based on people accepting a set of laws or rules. People obey an individual or group because they agree with the laws or rules on which their power rests. Rational legal authority operates within a **bureaucracy**, that is, an organisation with a hierarchy and a clear set of rules.
  - With charismatic authority, people obey a leader who they believe has extraordinary personal qualities that inspire them.

Marxist Perspectives on Power

- Marxist approaches see power as closely linked to social class relationships. The bourgeoisie's power is based on their ownership of the means of production. They use their power to exploit the proletariat.
- Political power comes from economic power so the bourgeoisie, by virtue of their economic power, also hold political power.

Key Thinker

Max Weber (1864–1920)

Key Point

Max Weber (1864–1920) is a key thinker, so it is important that you understand his ideas on power and authority.

Feminist Perspectives on Power

- Feminists see gender inequality as the most important source of division in society. Some feminists argue that society is patriarchal. In other words, it is controlled mainly by men who have considerable power within politics and the workplace. Men generally have a bigger share of wealth and social status.
- Women are under-represented among holders of political power, decision makers and within the top levels of the judiciary in Britain.

Walby on Patriarchy

- Walby (1990) defines patriarchy as a system of social structures and practices in which men dominate and exploit women. She highlights six patriarchal structures.
  1. **Paid employment:** women typically earn less than men and are excluded from better types of paid work.
  2. **The household:** husbands and partners exploit women by benefitting from their unpaid labour in the home.
  3. **Culture:** culture differentiates between masculinity and femininity (which is defined in terms of being sexually attractive to men).
  4. **Sexuality:** the **double standard** is an aspect of male dominance. For example, sexually active young women may be viewed as 'slags' while sexually active men may be admired.
  5. **Male violence against women:** male violence affects women's actions and is a form of power over them.
  6. **The state:** state policies are biased towards patriarchal interests. There has been little effort to improve women's position in the public sphere, for example in the workplace.

Everyday Power Relationships

- Power may be exercised in relationships between people in everyday settings such as homes, workplaces and classrooms. This is because people enter into power relationships when they try to control or influence other people's behaviour, or when others try to control them.
- Power relationships operate when there are inequalities in power between individuals and groups. They may operate, for instance, between children and parents, students and teachers, and the public and the police.

Women are under-represented amongst politicians.

Key Thinker

Sylvia Walby (1990)

Key Point

Sylvia Walby (1990) is a key thinker, so it is important that you understand her feminist approach to patriarchy, gender inequalities and women's inferior position in society.

Think about how Walby's ideas link to the topics of families, and crime and deviance.

Key Words

authority
traditional authority
rational legal authority
charismatic authority
monarchy
bureaucracy
double standard

Quick Test

1. Identify one similarity between authority and coercion.
2. What is power based on according to Marxist approaches?
3. Identify one patriarchal structure that Walby highlights.

Power and the State

You must be able to:

- Explain how power operates in the political process
- Explain different views on the role of the state and pressure groups.

Politics, Power and Power Relationships

- Politics involves the exercise of power and power relationships.

Key Point

In the UK, the state exercises authority over England, Northern Ireland, Scotland and Wales. Some state powers, however, have been passed to the Welsh Assembly, the Scottish Parliament and the Northern Ireland Assembly.

Term	What it means
Democracy	• In many nations, including the UK, the political system is based on democracy, i.e. government by the people. • In a democratic society, power is distributed widely and the government's power is based on rational legal authority rather than on coercion.
Dictatorship	• Political power is concentrated in the hands of a dictator who rules by force. • Censorship of the media (tight governmental control of media content) occurs under a dictatorship and propaganda campaigns are used to promote the dictatorship's views and win people's loyalty.
Representative democracy	• Citizens elect representatives who make political decisions on their behalf. • In UK general elections, voters in a constituency each cast one vote. Most candidates belong to a political party such as the Labour or Conservative Party. The candidate with the most votes becomes the Member of Parliament (MP) for that constituency and sits in the House of Commons. • This type of electoral system is known as first-past-the-post or winner takes all.
Proportional representation (PR)	• Seats are allocated according to the total number of votes that each party receives. • PR is used to elect Members of the European Parliament (MEPs).
The state	• A central part of the political process; refers to the various institutions (such as the police, civil service and judiciary) that organise and regulate society. • The role of state institutions is to make, implement and enforce laws.
The government of the UK	• Refers to MPs who are Ministers, selected by the Prime Minister, who is the leader of the governing political party. • Although the legal system, the military and the police force are all part of the state, they are independent of the government of the day.

The Role of the State

- There are two broad approaches to the study of power and the state: **pluralism** and the conflict approach. They differ in their views on the **distribution of power** in society and how power is used.

> The pluralist approach argues that a range of competing interests and **pressure groups** (or **interest groups**) exists in society. Political power is shared between these groups. No single group dominates decision-making or always gets its own way. The state's role is to act as a neutral referee, to regulate the different interests and serve the needs of all citizens.

> Sociologists from the Marxist or conflict approach argue that those in powerful positions within the state (such as top judges and senior civil servants) tend to come from privileged backgrounds. The owners of the means of production have power in capitalist society and the state's role is to protect their interests.

Key Point

Some social groups have more power than others. Power relationships are influenced by factors such as social class, gender, ethnicity and age.

The Role of Pressure Groups

- Pluralists argue that pressure groups, trade unions, **protest movements** and **new social movements** are crucial to democracy. Pressure groups, for example, allow like-minded citizens to join together and put forward their views.
- Protest movements organise **direct action** to protect the environment, for instance, or to focus attention on companies that avoid taxes. In this way, all opinions and interests can be represented and heard. Such groups provide opportunities for citizens to participate in the political process.
- The conflict view argues that society is based on conflicting interests between different groups.
- Some key groups, such as big business, have enough power, staff and financial resources to be able to influence government policies.
- Some groups' power is based on their ownership of property, wealth and resources. This gives them status and they can exert more influence on policy makers than other groups and dominate decision-making.

Some trade unions have over one million members.

Key Words

democracy
dictatorship
censorship
propaganda
constituency
political party
Member of Parliament
first-past-the-post
proportional
 representation
Prime Minister
pluralism
distribution of power
pressure groups
interest groups
protest movements
new social movements
direct action

Quick Test

1. Identify one factor that influences power relationships.
2. What term refers to the institutions that organise and regulate society?
3. How is power distributed according to the pluralist view?

An Introduction to Crime and Deviance

1. Identify **one** agency of informal social control and explain how you would investigate this agency using questionnaires.   [4]

Functionalist and Interactionist Perspectives on Crime and Deviance

2. Describe a deviant career as outlined by Becker.   [3]

....

....

....

....

Marxist and Feminist Explanations of Crime and Deviance

3 Describe the double deviance experienced by some women within the criminal justice system. [3]

....

....

....

....

....

....

....

....

Statistical Data on the Extent of Crime

4 Describe **one** example of corporate crime. [3]

....

....

....

....

....

Factors Affecting Criminal and Deviant Behaviour

5 Describe the status frustration experienced by some young people at school. [3]

Other Factors Affecting Criminal and Deviant Behaviour

6 Identify and explain **one** reason why there are more men than women in prison in the UK. [4]

7 Describe the gender deal outlined by Carlen. [3]

The Media and Public Debates over Crime

8 Which term is used by sociologists to describe the media's ability to focus public attention on particular topics, and direct public discussion onto these topics? Shade **one** box only. [1]

A   News values   ◯

B   Gatekeeping   ◯

C   Agenda setting   ◯

D   Scapegoating   ◯

An Introduction to Social Stratification

1 Describe **one** example of a system of social stratification. [3]

Different Views of Social Class

2 Describe the experience of alienation at work. [3]

Factors Affecting Life Chances

3 Identify and explain **one** reason why women, on average, earn less than men. [4]

_____

_____

_____

_____

_____

_____

_____

_____

_____

_____

Studies of Affluent Workers

4 Identify and explain **one** advantage of using structured interviews to investigate social mobility in the UK. [4]

_____

_____

_____

_____

_____

Wealth, Income and Poverty

5 Identify and describe **one** way of defining poverty.   [3]

Different Explanations of Poverty

6 Describe the cycle of deprivation experienced by some families.   [3]

....

....

....

....

....

Power and Authority

7 Identify **one** group that has power in British society and describe their power. [3]

....

....

....

....

....

....

....

....

Power and the State

8 Which of the following is used by sociologists to refer to the various institutions that organise and regulate society? Shade **one** box only. [1]

A Civil service ◯

B Judiciary ◯

C State ◯

D Government ◯

An Introduction to Social Stratification

1   Describe what sociologists mean by social inequality.   [3]

Different Views of Social Class

2   Identify and explain **one** way of measuring social class.   [4]

....

....

Factors Affecting Life Chances

3 Identify and describe **one** example of how life chances differ between social classes. [3]

....

....

....

....

....

....

....

Studies of Affluent Workers

4 Describe the 'privatised instrumentalism' that people in some families may experience. [3]

....

....

....

....

....

....

....

Wealth, Income and Poverty

5   Which term is commonly used by sociologists to describe a state of poverty in which people cannot afford to meet the general standard of living of most others in their society? Shade **one** box only.

[1]

A   Environmental poverty   **B**   Subjective poverty

C   Absolute poverty   **D**   Relative poverty ◯

Different Explanations of Poverty

6   Identify and describe **one** characteristic of the underclass, as outlined by Charles Murray.

[3]

Power and Authority

7   Identify and describe **one** type of authority.

[3]

Power and the State

8 Identify and explain **one** advantage of using covert observation to investigate a protest movement in the UK.

[4]

Mixed Questions

1 Which term is used by sociologists to describe an informed guess or hunch? Shade **one** box only.   [1]

A   Aim   ◯

B   Question   ◯

C   Hypothesis   ◯

D   Theory   ◯

2 Identify **one** ethical issue that you would need to consider when investigating the relationship between parents and teenagers, and explain how you would deal with this issue in your investigation.   [4]

3 Discuss how far sociologists agree that conjugal roles have changed in Britain over the last 40 years as a result of feminism.

[12]

Continue your answer on a separate piece of paper.

Mixed Questions

4 Which term is commonly used by sociologists to describe middle class parents' knowledge of how the education system works and how to work it to their advantage? Shade **one** box only. [1]

A Economic capital ◯

B Social capital ◯

C Cultural capital ◯

D Cultural deprivation ◯

5 Identify and explain **one** disadvantage of using unstructured interviews to investigate students' experiences of racism within higher education. [4]

6 Discuss how far sociologists agree that school-based factors are the most important issue in explaining differences in students' educational achievements. [12]

Continue your answer on a separate piece of paper.

Mixed Questions

7 Which of the following is described by sociologists as an informal agency of social control?
Shade **one** box only. [1]

A Crown court ◯

B Prison service ◯

C Religion ◯

D Role conflict ◯

8 Identify and explain **one** disadvantage of using participant observation to investigate a criminal sub-culture. [4]

....

....

....

....

....

....

....

....

....

....

9 Discuss how far sociologists agree that peer pressure is the main reason for deviance among young people.

[12]

_____

_____

_____

_____

_____

_____

_____

_____

_____

_____

_____

_____

_____

_____

_____

_____

Continue your answer on a separate piece of paper.

Mixed Questions

10 Which term is commonly used by sociologists to describe a class of privileged people who have hereditary titles such as Duke or Lady? Shade **one** box only. [1]

A Aristocracy   ◯

B Bourgeoisie   ◯

C Oligarchy   ◯

D Elite   ◯

11 Identify and explain **one** disadvantage of using a longitudinal study to investigate social mobility. [4]

12 Discuss how far sociologists agree that the behaviour of individuals and families is the most important reason for the existence of poverty in the UK. [12]

Continue your answer on a separate piece of paper.

Answers

Pages 6–7
1. **Any one from:** socialisation; labelling; social control.
2. False: norms provide these guidelines.
3. Socialisation

Pages 8–9
1. **Any one from:** the bourgeoisie own the means of production/ the proletariat own only their labour power; the bourgeoisie are the ruling class/the proletariat are the subject class.
2. **Any one from:** to bring people together; to reinforce the values and beliefs of the majority; to contribute to social cohesion.

Pages 10–11
1. **Any one from:** they define class in terms of economic factors; they see ownership and non-ownership as the most important basis of class divisions.
2. Functionalism sees society as based on consensus; Marxism sees it as based on conflict.
3. They are both conflict theories/see society as based on conflict.

Pages 12–13
1. True
2. False: this is true for systematic sampling.
3. False: this is true for snowball sampling.

Pages 14–15
1. **Any one from:** they can be answered quickly; responses are relatively easy to process by computer; they provide quantitative data.
2. **Any one from:** relatively expensive; relatively time-consuming; difficult to stay in contact with the original sample over time; participants may withdraw.
3. **Any one from:** they are based on a standardised set of questions; both produce quantitative data; both enable replication; both enable generalisations.

Pages 16–17
1. When the interview situation influences interviewees' responses.
2. This occurs in a study based on observation when the researcher's known presence influences research participants' behaviour.

Pages 18–19
1. False: content analysis generates quantitative data from qualitative sources.
2. False: crime rates are less likely than birth rates to be valid.

The Sociological Approach
1. **Suggested answer:** A norm gives people guidelines on appropriate behaviour in a specific setting. For example, in a supermarket queue the norm is to form an orderly line at the cash desk without pushing in. Without this norm, supermarkets would not run smoothly and social order could break down. **[Maximum 3 marks]**

The Key Ideas of Marx and Durkheim
2. **Suggested answer:** If a society has social cohesion, its people share a set of values (known as value consensus), beliefs and attitudes. This helps to bring people together as a whole and provides stability and order in society. **[Maximum 3 marks]**

Other Sociological Approaches
3. **Suggested answer:** Patriarchy literally means 'rule of the father'. Feminist sociologists define patriarchy as male control over women. One example of patriarchy in a nuclear family is the husband having power and control in decisions about how the family income is spent. **[Maximum 3 marks]**

Research Design
4. **Suggested answer:** To do research ethically, sociologists must obtain informed consent (or permission) from research participants. This involves explaining to participants what the research is about and why it is being carried out. The participant can then agree (or refuse) to take part and this agreement must be based on having information about the study. **[Maximum 3 marks]**

Quantitative Methods
5. **Example answer:** One advantage is that comparisons can be made. **[1]** All respondents answer the same questions about their experiences of crime and statistical data can be collected from a large sample. This means that comparisons can be made between social groups (e.g. Male and female victims of crime or young and older victims) or between geographical areas. **[3] Other possible advantages:** Measurement of trends in victimisation over time; to collect statistics to compare with police-recorded crime statistics; the benefits of quantitative data – **1 mark for a relevant advantage and 3 marks for explaining this advantage.**

Qualitative Methods
6. **Example answer:** One advantage is that the observer gets a first-hand account through the collection of primary data. **[1]** An observer is present in the classroom to see action as it unfolds in real time and does not have to rely on what teachers and students tell them in interviews afterwards about classroom interaction. **[3] Other possible advantages:** Qualitative data can be obtained to give a detailed insight into classroom interaction; the observer is less likely to become too involved if they do not participate; an observer may be more objective than a participant observer – **1 mark for a relevant advantage and 3 marks for explaining this advantage.**

Secondary Sources of Data
7. **Example answer:** It involves subjective judgements. **[1]** The researcher must construct a set of categories before coding all sections of the magazines' contents. Coding involves subjective judgements (e.g. one researcher might see a particular image as sexist while others see it as poking fun at sexism). The researcher could end up with a lot of statistical data that lacks validity. **[3] Other possible disadvantages:** Time-consuming; laborious – **1 mark for a relevant disadvantage and 3 marks for explaining this disadvantage.**

Pages 24–25
1. A literature review/secondary sources/drew on other sociologists' work.
2. Different types of diversity in families in Britain.
3. True

Pages 26–27
1. Functionalism
2. The 1950s
3. False: Parsons identified two basic and vital functions.

Pages 28–29
1. **Any one from:** economic function; reproduces social class inequalities over time; socialisation.
2. It is unpaid/seen as separate from the world of paid work.

3. **Any one from:** Functionalism sees the nuclear family as meeting the needs of individuals and society; Marxism sees it as meeting the needs of capitalism. Functionalism sees the nuclear family as inevitable; Marxism argues that it should be abolished.

Pages 30–31
1. Existing research/a literature review/secondary sources/drew on other sociologists' work.
2. Patriarchy in families; economic exploitation in families.
3. **Any one from:** they both adopt a conflict approach; both see the family as a source of inequality and oppression; both are critical of functionalism.

Pages 32–33
1. Questionnaire survey/structured interview.
2. **Any one from:** Functionalism sees conjugal roles as fair, with tasks equally divided, but feminism sees conjugal roles as unfair and unequal. Functionalism sees the division of labour as based on biological differences between the sexes, but feminism sees it as socially constructed.
3. **Any one from:** with joint conjugal roles, domestic tasks are not gendered but with segregated conjugal roles, domestic tasks are divided by gender; with joint conjugal roles, the partners share leisure activities but with segregated conjugal roles, they do not share leisure time.

Pages 34–35
1. False: they study the family from a functionalist perspective.
2. An arranged marriage is based on consent/choice; a forced marriage is based on coercion/lack of choice.
3. The average number of years a person can expect to live.

Pages 36–37
1. Decreased
2. **Any one from:** the increase in divorce; changing views on families and marriage/more freedom in choice of relationships; single motherhood is more socially acceptable.
3. False: family size has decreased, on average.

Pages 38–39
1. False: polygamy describes the practice of having more than one spouse at once.
2. **Any one from:** changing social attitudes to sex outside marriage; the high cost of weddings; secularisation.
3. **Any one from:** they may live in a lone-parent family – if so, they may be more at risk of poverty; they may have to adjust to life in a reconstituted family; they may see less of/lose contact with their father; they may see less of/lose contact with some relatives.

Pages 40–43 Review Questions

The Sociological Approach
1. **Suggested answer:** Refers to a society's whole way of life including its language, values, norms, customs and beliefs. It can also refer to a particular group such as a youth culture (for example, punks or hippies) who share an identity and a style of dress. **[Maximum 3 marks]**
2. **B**

The Key Ideas of Marx and Durkheim
3. **Suggested answer:** The materials (both raw materials and tools) that people use in the production process. For example, under capitalism, the means of production include capital, factories, property, machinery and land, and are owned by the bourgeoisie. **[Maximum 3 marks]**

Other Sociological Approaches
4. **Suggested answer:** Functionalism sees society as based on value consensus, in that people broadly agree on society's values and norms and are willing to conform to them. Value consensus comes about through socialisation. If people agree on values, then society is likely to run smoothly. **[Maximum 3 marks]**

Research Design
5. **Suggested answer:** A subgroup (sample) that is typical (representative) of the wider population (e.g. it has the same proportion of men and women as the population); it is a mirror image but a smaller version of the population. Sociologists must use a representative sample if they want to make generalisations. **[Maximum 3 marks]**
6. **C**

Quantitative Methods
7. **B**

Qualitative Methods
8. **Example answer:** One advantage is gaining extra insights into the fear of crime. **[1]** In a focus group, the researcher can explore how people from one community respond to each other's views on the fear of crime and how far they agree with each other. This would generate insights into the fear of crime that would not emerge with individual interviews. **[3] Other possible answers:** Accessing a range of contrasting views on why some people, but not others, fear crime in a community; interviewees may feel empowered or more comfortable in a group setting and therefore more likely to open up – **1 mark for a relevant advantage and 3 marks for explaining this advantage.**

Secondary Sources of Data
9. **Example answer:** They exclude unreported incidents of domestic violence. **[1]** Victims of domestic violence might not report it to the police because they fear the consequences. Domestic violence is likely to be under-reported, so the police-recorded statistics will provide an incomplete picture of its extent. So sociologists cannot rely on these statistics as an accurate measure of domestic violence. **[3] Other possible answers:** The exclusion of unrecorded incidents; the lack of qualitative detail about the nature of domestic violence – **1 mark for a relevant disadvantage and 3 marks for explaining this disadvantage.**

Pages 44–47 Practice Questions

Different Family Forms
1. **Example answer:** A nuclear family – a family made up of a father, mother and their dependent child or children. It is two-generational and family members live together in the same household. The parents may be married or cohabiting. **[Maximum 3 marks]**

The Functions of Families
2. **B**

Marxist Perspectives on Families
3. **Suggested answer:** The private sphere refers to the home and family life as opposed to the public sphere of the economy and paid work. According to Zaretsky, industrial capitalism led to the separation of these two spheres and women became responsible for the private sphere, including family members' emotional well-being. **[Maximum 3 marks]**

Feminist and Other Critical Views of Families
4. **Suggested answer:** Canalisation describes the way parents channel their children's interests into toys, games and other activities that are seen as gender appropriate. So parents (and other people) buy toys such as baby dolls and prams for girls, and action man and guns for boys. This channelling is part of the gender socialisation process and helps to reproduce gender inequalities over time. **[Maximum 3 marks]**

Conjugal Role Relationships
5. **Suggested answer:** A symmetrical family is a nuclear family in which conjugal relationships are opposite but similar. The spouses perform different tasks but each makes a similar contribution to the home. Decision-making, including financial decisions, is more shared and family members are home-centred, sharing much of their leisure time. **[Maximum 3 marks]**

Changing Relationships Within Families

6. **Suggested answer:** Young and Willmott (1973) developed this principle when studying changing family life since the mid-19th century. This suggests that many social changes (e.g. in values and attitudes) start at the top of the social class system and work downwards. Changes in family life filter down from the middle class into the working class. **[Maximum 3 marks]**

Changing Family and Household Structures

7. **Example answer:** Social attitudes towards lone-parents have changed. **[1]** It is now more socially acceptable for single women to have children without a partner. Single and divorced women can use new technologies (e.g. IVF at a fertility clinic) to become single mothers by choice without the need for a male partner. **[3] Other possible answers:** the increase in divorce; changes in how people view the family, marriage and intimate relationships – **1 mark for identifying a relevant reason and 3 marks for explaining this reason.**

Marriage and Divorce

8. **Example answer:** Secularisation, **[1]** the decline in the influence of religion in society. Christian churches, for example, have fewer members compared to the 1970s. More people now have a civil ceremony in a registry office or other licensed venue rather than a church wedding. Fewer people take sacred vows to stay together 'till death us do part' so the religious barrier to divorce has weakened. **[3] Other possible factors:** Legal changes; changing social attitudes towards divorce; the changing status of women; higher expectations of marriage – **1 mark for identifying a relevant factor and 3 marks for explaining this factor.**

Pages 48–63 Revise Questions

Pages 48–49
1. False: ascribed status is fixed at birth.
2. False: universalistic standards apply to everyone in the same way.

Pages 50–51
1. **Any one from:** Functionalism sees education as meritocratic; Marxism sees it as favouring the privileged. Education prepares young people for work in industrial society (functionalism); education prepares them for exploitation under capitalism (Marxism). They differ in their view of the role of socialisation within education.
2. Hidden curriculum
3. Intelligence quotient (IQ)

Pages 52–53
1. True
2. False: comprehensive schools are not selective.
3. **Any one from:** public schools (such as Eton and Harrow) are older and have a longer history than other private schools; public schools charge higher fees (are more expensive) than other private schools; public schools are seen as more prestigious and more exclusive than other private schools.

Pages 54–55
1. False: material deprivation refers to financial issues.
2. True

Pages 56–57
1. Small-scale interactions
2. **Any one from:** school registers; school records.
3. **Any one from:** labelling; change in students' behaviour; development of an anti-school sub-culture; teachers' different expectations of each band; bands taught differently, self-fulfilling prophecy.

Pages 58–59
1. Ethnocentric
2. Institutional racism
3. **Any one from:** material deprivation; lacking the right sort of cultural capital; other cultural factors; parental values.

Pages 60–61
1. **Any one from:** the impact of feminism; equal opportunities policies in schools; the impact of legislation; the introduction of the National Curriculum.
2. True
3. **Any one from:** gender socialisation at home; gender socialisation at school; gender stereotyping in textbooks; teacher attitudes to gender; the gendered curriculum.

Pages 62–63
1. **Any one from:** membership discourages students from working hard; they reject learning; they do not value qualifications/education/academic study; membership influences teacher expectations.
2. Bowles and Gintis saw schools as turning working-class students into passive conformists but Willis's lads opposed the school and resisted authority.
3. False: blue-collar work involves skilled, semi-skilled or unskilled manual work and is performed by blue-collar workers.

Pages 64–67 Review Questions

Different Family Forms
1. **Suggested answer:** The range of different family types found in Britain today. Examples of these different types include nuclear, extended, lone-parent, same-sex and blended families. Aspects of family diversity also include differences between families based on factors such as social class, culture and cohort. **[Maximum 3 marks]**

The Functions of Families
2. **Example answer:** Primary socialisation of children **[1]** – early childhood learning during which babies and infants learn basic behaviour patterns, language and skills for later life. Parsons argues that through the process of primary socialisation in nuclear families, children learn the culture of their society and come to accept society's shared values. **[3] Other possible functions:** Stabilisation of adult personalities, the sexual, reproductive, economic and educational functions – **1 mark for a relevant function and 3 marks for explaining this function.**

The Marxist Perspective on Families
3. **Suggested answer:** The public sphere refers to the world of the economy and paid work, where commodities and profits are produced, as opposed to the private sphere of the home and family life. Zaretsky argued that industrial capitalism led to the separation of these two spheres and men took on a role in the public sphere. **[Maximum 3 marks]**

Feminist and Other Critical Views on Families
4. B

Conjugal Role Relationships
5. **Suggested answer:** According to Parsons, a functionalist sociologist, the expressive role refers to the woman's role in a nuclear family as housewife and mother, with responsibility for the household and for providing emotional support to family members. By contrast, men have the instrumental role within the workplace. **[Maximum 3 marks]**

Changing Relationships Within Families
6. **Example answer:** Relationships are less authoritarian today compared to 100 years ago. **[1]** There is now less emphasis on discipline and parental authority over children and more emphasis on individual freedom and democracy. Children are seen as important family members whose views are taken seriously. **[3] Other possible ways:** A move to child-centred relationships; a move to closer, warmer emotional relationships; child-rearing is no longer based on economic factors – **1 mark for a relevant way and 3 marks for explaining this way.**

Changing Family and Household Structures
7. **Suggested answer:** All individuals have several roles at once, for example parent, employee, friend and volunteer. Role conflict occurs when the demands of one of these roles (e.g. a parent in full-time employment whose child has just broken her arm) clash with the demands of another (e.g. the parent has an important job interview that morning). **[Maximum 3 marks]**

Marriage and Divorce

8. **Suggested answer:** The process whereby religion loses its influence or significance in a society. For example, religion no longer plays a key role in politics or in education and is no longer an important agency of socialisation or social control. **[Maximum 3 marks]**

Pages 68–71 Practice Questions

The Role of Education from a Functionalist Perspective

1. **Suggested answer:** Social mobility. Upward or downward mobility is possible in a meritocracy because people achieve their social position based on their individual talents and abilities rather than status being ascribed at birth. **[Maximum 3 marks]**

The Marxist Approach to Education

2. **Suggested answer:** The values that students learn indirectly at school that are not taught formally within lessons as part of the national curriculum. One aspect involves valuing punctuality and conformity, which students learn about through the school rules. **[Maximum 3 marks]**

Different Types of School

3. A

Social Class and Educational Achievement

4. **Suggested answer:** The policy of introducing market forces (such as competition and choice) into education to raise standards. Schools must promote themselves in order to compete to attract students, and parents can compare schools' performances by looking at league tables. **[Maximum 3 marks]**

The Impact of School Processes on Working-Class Students' Achievements

5. **Suggested answer:** Streaming, whereby students are placed in a class based on their general ability and are taught in this class for most subjects. Some teachers may have low expectations of students in the lower streams and give them less encouragement, so students give up trying and underachieve academically. In this case, streaming leads to a self-fulfilling prophecy. **[Maximum 3 marks]**

Ethnicity and Educational Achievement

6. **Suggested answer:** Biased towards white, European culture. For example, the national curriculum is seen as ethnocentric because it tends to exclude non-European languages, literature, art and music. Subjects like history, for instance, may be taught from a British or European perspective. **[Maximum 3 marks]**

Gender and Educational Achievement

7. **Example answer:** The impact of feminism. **[1]** Feminism has resulted in changing social expectations about gender roles. In the past, men were usually expected to be breadwinners while women were expected to be homemakers. Today, girls are more focused on paid employment, careers and financial independence. They see educational achievement as a route to these. **[3] Other possible reasons:** The introduction of the National Curriculum; legislation such as the Sex Discrimination Act; equal opportunities policies in schools; girl-friendly schooling, teaching methods and assessment that favour girls' learning styles – **1 mark for identifying a relevant reason and 3 marks for explaining this reason.**

Perspectives on the Counter-School Culture

8. **Example answer:** Belonging to a counter-school culture may encourage anti-learning attitudes among its members. **[1]** Paul Willis's case study showed that boys in an anti-school culture opposed their teachers' authority and did not value academic learning. This could affect students' progress and achievement if peer pressure means they make no effort to learn or improve. **[3] Other possible ways:** Being placed in the lower streams; low teacher expectations; labelling; self-fulfilling prophecy; peer pressure to truant – **1 mark for identifying a relevant way and 3 marks for explaining this way.**

Pages 72–85 Revise Questions

Pages 72–73 Quick Test

1. **Any one from:** they both involve breaking rules; they are both subject to social control.
2. Functionalism sees social order as based on agreement about the rules; Marxism sees it as enforced/based on power.
3. Formal social control is based on written rules/laws/enforced by the state; informal social control is based on unwritten rules/ norms/enforced via social pressure.

Pages 74–75

1. True
2. Culture/cultural values/society/socialisation
3. Social groups/society

Pages 76–77

1. They are both structural approaches.
2. **Any one from:** they both see the criminal justice system (CJS) as unfair; both critical of the CJS; both critical of functionalism.

Pages 78–79

1. **Any one from:** they lack validity; they are socially constructed; they exclude undiscovered/unreported/unrecorded crime/the 'dark figure' of crime; they reflect labelling processes; they reflect class/gender bias.
2. False: self-report studies question respondents about their involvement in crime.

Pages 80–81

1. False: they are examples of corporate crime.
2. Cohen focuses on males/his explanation does not address delinquency among girls.
3. Status frustration/membership of a delinquent sub-culture/the education system/social class/gender/age.

Pages 82–83

1. **Any one from:** the class deal; the gender deal; girls are more closely supervised than boys.
2. **Any one from:** they are more likely to be stopped and searched by the police; higher rates of unemployment, poverty and deprivation; policing and bias within the CJS; institutional racism.

Pages 84–85

1. **Any three from:** hoodies/mods/rockers/refugees/asylum seekers/ benefit cheats/single mothers.
2. Media professionals and owners who decide what gets covered and how.
3. An individual or group that gets blamed for something that is not their fault.

Pages 86–89 Review Questions

The Role of Education from a Functionalist Perspective

1. **Suggested answer:** With achieved status, a person's social position is based on their individual talents and abilities rather than being fixed at birth. In the class system, upward social mobility is possible, so a talented working-class student can work hard at school, achieve good exam results, go to university, get a professional job and move up into the middle class. **[Maximum 3 marks]**

The Marxist Approach to Education

2. D

Different Types of School

3. **Suggested answer:** Private schools are not funded by the state. They are independent of the state and do not have to follow the national curriculum. Most parents pay fees for their children to attend these schools. Many private schools are selective, have an entrance exam and market their academic ethos and extra-curricular activities. **[Maximum 3 marks]**

Social Class and Educational Achievement

4. **Suggested answer:** One example is the increased competition between schools in order to attract parents and students (the customers). The idea is that this will raise standards in education and improve schools. So schools now operate as businesses, and have glossy prospectuses and marketing staff. **[Maximum 3 marks]**

The Impact of School Processes on Working-Class Students' Achievements

5. **Suggested answer:** If students are labelled as 'less able' (e.g. by being placed in the lower streams), they may come to see themselves as less able. As a result, they think there is no point in making an effort to improve, and underachieve. In this case, the labelling is linked to a self-fulfilling prophecy. **[Maximum 3 marks]**

Ethnicity and Educational Achievement

6. **Suggested answer:** The members of an ethnic group share an identity based on their cultural characteristics or traditions, such as a religion or language. Irish people are one example of an ethnic group in Britain. They share an Irish culture, identity, the experience of migration and may share a religion. **[Maximum 3 marks]** (Any other relevant example credited.)

Gender and Educational Achievement

7. **Example answer:** Schools have become too girl-friendly. **[1]** Changes to the exam system and the way courses are assessed, such as modular assessment, oral assessment, continuous assessment and coursework, may favour girls and discriminate against boys. Boys are forced to learn in ways that do not suit them. **[3] Other possible reasons:** The anti-school sub-culture; laddish culture; peer pressure; crisis of masculinity; the feminisation of primary schooling – **1 mark for a relevant reason and 3 marks for explaining this reason.**

Perspectives on the Counter-School Culture

8. **Example answer:** Inflexibility as a method. **[1]** Questionnaires are based on a standardised, pre-structured set of questions. As a result, they do not give the researcher any flexibility to follow a new line of enquiry into counter-school cultures if the questions are not included on the schedule. **[3] Other possible disadvantages:** Not collecting in-depth qualitative data; low response rate; members of a counter-school culture may not take the questionnaire seriously, lowering the validity of the findings – **1 mark for a relevant disadvantage and 3 marks for explaining this disadvantage.**

Pages 90–93 **Practice Questions**

An Introduction to Crime and Deviance

1. **Suggested answer:** Deviance refers to behaviour that does not conform to society's norms and values. People value their privacy, so it would be deviant to invade someone's privacy by reading their text messages and emails on their mobile phone without their permission. **[Maximum 3 marks]** (Any other relevant example credited.)

Functionalist and Interactionist Perspectives on Crime and Deviance

2. **Suggested answer:** The status of 'drug addict' could become a master status. If a person is caught using drugs and labelled a deviant, this label can change how others see them. They are now seen as 'the local junkie'. This new status becomes a master status if it becomes the dominant status and overrides all their other statuses such as son, father, brother or employee. **[Maximum 3 marks]** (Any other relevant example credited.)

Marxist and Feminist Explanations of Crime and Deviance

3. **Suggested answer:** White-collar crimes involve criminal offences carried out by people who have relatively high status positions such as accountants or lawyers during their work. One example would be a solicitor who uses his status and position of trust in a law firm to defraud clients and steal money from them. **[Maximum 3 marks]** (Any other relevant example credited.)

Statistical Data on the Extent of Crime

4. **Suggested answer:** An example is the Crime Survey for England and Wales; a questionnaire or structured interview that examines people's experiences as victims of particular crimes and whether they reported them to the police. It provides statistics that can be compared with police-recorded crime statistics to investigate unrecorded crime. **[Maximum 3 marks]**

5. A

Factors Affecting Criminal and Deviant Behaviour

6. **Example answer:** Status frustration and sub-culture. **[1]** Albert Cohen linked delinquency such as vandalism and violence among working-class boys to status frustration at school. These boys fail to meet middle-class expectations at school and respond to this by joining a delinquent sub-culture. They commit crime to gain status within the gang. **[3] Other possible reasons:** Laddish culture; peer pressure; inadequate socialisation – **1 mark for a relevant reason and 3 marks for explaining this reason.**

Other Factors Affecting Criminal and Deviant Behaviour

7. **Suggested answer:** This is the idea that people who work within the criminal justice system – such as police officers and magistrates – treat women (particularly those who conform to feminine stereotypes) more leniently than men, e.g. during arrest and sentencing. Women are seen as needing help rather than punishment. **[Maximum 3 marks]**

The Media and Public Debates Over Crime

8. **Example answer:** Flexibility of this research method. **[1]** Unstructured interviews are based on a few prompts or points rather than a pre-set schedule of questions. They are flexible, so the interviewer can ask follow-up questions about an interviewee's concerns, and probe replies. This method may uncover fresh issues about people's concerns over youth crime that would not have been anticipated in advance. **[3] Other possible advantages:** Obtaining detailed qualitative data; avoiding the problem of a low response rate; obtaining valid data; allows rapport to develop between interviewer and interviewee – **1 mark for a relevant advantage and 3 marks for explaining this advantage.**

Pages 94–109 **Revise Questions**

Pages 94–95

1. True
2. False: social stratification refers to the division of society into a hierarchy of layers, with the most privileged at the top and the least privileged at the bottom.
3. To match the most talented people to the most important jobs.

Pages 96–97

1. Marx saw status as arising from class divisions; Weber saw class and status as two separate aspects of stratification.
2. Similar life chances/similar market situation.
3. It is linked to levels of pay, working conditions and status.

Pages 98–99

1. **Any one from:** through legislation/laws; regulations against age discrimination.
2. False: the glass ceiling refers to an invisible barrier to women's promotion at work.

Pages 100–101

1. True
2. True

Pages 102–103

1. **Any one from:** low incomes; subjective poverty; environmental poverty; relative deprivation.
2. **Any one from:** Some items do not necessarily measure deprivation; the index is inadequate so the statistics will be questionable.

Pages 104–105

1. **Any one from:** New Right approach; the culture of poverty; the cycle of deprivation.
2. New Right.

Pages 106–107

1. They are both sources of power.
2. Ownership of the means of production/social class relationships/economic factors.
3. **Any one from:** paid employment; the household; culture; sexuality; male violence; the state.

Pages 108–109

1. **Any one from:** social class; gender; ethnicity; age.
2. The state.
3. It is shared between different groups.

Pages 110–113 Review Questions

An Introduction to Crime and Deviance

1. **Example answer:** Families. **[1]** I would design a questionnaire to ask family members (parents and children) about how social control works in their family. Next, I would identify a representative or typical sample of families and obtain family members' informed consent before asking them to complete the questionnaire. I would then analyse the data, looking for any patterns in what respondents say about informal social control in their family and any connections between variables such as the parents' social class and their attitudes to discipline. **[3] Other possible agencies:** Religions; peer groups; workplaces – **1 mark for identifying a relevant agency and 3 marks for explaining how you would investigate this agency using questionnaires.**

Functionalist and Interactionist Perspectives on Crime and Deviance

2. **Suggested answer:** Becker saw a deviant career as a process or a set of steps that some individuals go through as they come to see themselves as deviant (or outsiders) and get more drawn into deviant activities. It involves being publicly labelled as a deviant, joining a deviant sub-culture and making deviance a way of life. **[Maximum 3 marks]**

Marxist and Feminist Explanations of Crime and Deviance

3. **Suggested answer:** Double deviance is the idea that female offenders are treated more harshly than male offenders within the criminal justice system because their behaviour is viewed as deviant in two ways: it is seen not only as illegal but also as unfeminine because it does not conform to gender expectations. **[Maximum 3 marks]**

Statistical Data on the Extent of Crime

4. **Suggested answer:** Corporate crime is crime committed by corporations or large companies, or by employees on behalf of these companies. One example is offences against consumers such as the sale of unfit food (e.g. selling horsemeat in bulk but marketing it as beef) or unsafe products. **[Maximum 3 marks]**

Factors Affecting Criminal and Deviant Behaviour

5. **Suggested answer:** Status frustration refers to the feelings of anger or annoyance that people experience when denied the opportunity to get social status. Albert Cohen argued that working-class boys feel frustrated at school because they cannot compete with middle-class boys to get status through academic achievement. They respond by gaining status within a delinquent sub-culture. **[Maximum 3 marks]**

Other Factors Affecting Criminal and Deviant Behaviour

6. **Example answer:** Gender socialisation. **[1]** In general, from an early age, girls are socialised to be more passive and boys are socialised to be more active. If males conform to society's view of masculinity, they may be under pressure to act macho and tough. They are more likely to get into conflicts with the police or get involved in violent or serious crime than females and to end up in prison. **[3] Other possible reasons:** Women have fewer opportunities to commit crime; chivalry thesis; men commit more serious crimes – **1 mark for identifying a relevant reason and 3 marks for explaining this reason.**

7. **Suggested answer:** Pat Carlen argued that working-class women sign up for the gender deal (as well as the class deal). This deal offers them material and emotional rewards in return for living with a male breadwinner within the family. The gender deal breaks down if the rewards are not available or not worth it. **[Maximum 3 marks]**

The Media and Public Debates over Crime

8. C

Pages 114–117 Practice Questions

An Introduction to Social Stratification

1. **Suggested answer:** Social stratification is the division of society into a hierarchy of unequal strata. One example is social class which is based on economic factors such as occupation and income. The upper class make up the top layer and have much more wealth, status and power than the middle- and working-class strata, but social mobility is possible. **[Maximum 3 marks]**

Different Views of Social Class

2. **Suggested answer:** Marxist sociologists use this term to describe the proletariat's feeling of being cut off (or estranged) from their work under capitalism. This is because they have no control over the production process itself or over the products of their labour. **[Maximum 3 marks]**

Factors Affecting Life Chances

3. **Example answer:** Women's triple shift. **[1]** Many women in paid employment are also responsible for domestic labour and for emotion work (making their children and partners feel good) within their family. This extra burden makes it difficult for women to compete on equal terms with men for well-paid jobs and promotion. **[3] Other possible reasons:** The glass ceiling; sex discrimination in the workplace; inadequate childcare provision; more likely to work part-time – **1 mark for a relevant reason and 3 marks for explaining this reason.**

Studies of Affluent Workers

4. **Example answer:** Quantitative data. **[1]** Structured interviews ask standardised questions and statistical data can be gathered from closed questions about social mobility. The researcher can compare responses to each question, look for connections between variables and patterns in the data, and build up a picture of the nature and extent of social mobility in the UK. **[3] Other possible advantages:** Large sample size; reliability; generalisations from a large and representative sample – **1 mark for a relevant advantage and 3 marks for explaining this advantage.**

Wealth, Income and Poverty

5. **Suggested answer:** Absolute poverty: a person experiences absolute poverty when their income is so low that they cannot afford the basic necessities or minimum essentials that are needed to survive, such as food and shelter. **[Maximum 3 marks]**

Different Explanations of Poverty

6. **Suggested answer:** The cycle of deprivation shows how poverty and deprivation get passed on from parents to children in families. In this view, children who are born into poor families experience material and cultural deprivation. As adults, they live in poverty and go on to become the parents of deprived children. **[Maximum 3 marks]**

Power and Authority

7. **Suggested answer:** Many feminist sociologists argue that men have power and control over women in patriarchal society. In Britain, men control more of the wealth and hold most top positions within the state, industry and business. In families, they are more likely to control the finances and decision-making. **[Maximum 3 marks]**

Power and the State

8. C

An Introduction to Social Stratification

1. **Suggested answer:** Social inequality refers to the uneven distribution of resources such as income, wealth and power in society, as well as the unequal distribution of opportunities, e.g. between different social classes and ethnic groups within education. **[Maximum 3 marks]**

Different Views of Social Class

2. **Example answer:** Occupation. **[1]** People's social class can be measured by their current occupation or job – in other words, how they earn a living. Occupation is used because it relates to factors such as people's income (annual salary or hourly pay), qualifications required to do the job, working conditions, social status and their life chances, linked, for instance, to health and life expectancy. **[3] Other possible ways:** People's subjective assessments of their class; previous job if unemployed or retired; ownership or non-ownership of the means of production – **1 mark for a relevant way and 3 marks for explaining this way.**

Factors Affecting Life Chances

3. **Suggested answer:** Life chances are people's chances of achieving positive or negative outcomes as they go through life. The middle class have better health and life expectancy than the working class because they tend to have higher incomes and are more able to afford private health care, or they get private health insurance through work. **[Maximum 3 marks]**

Studies of Affluent Workers

4. **Suggested answer:** This involves living in a privatised nuclear family in which relationships centre on the home rather than on work. Paid work is just a means to an end (e.g. to maintain a good standard of living) rather than an end in itself (e.g. job satisfaction). **[Maximum 3 marks]**

Wealth, Income and Poverty

5. D

Different Explanations of Poverty

6. **Suggested answer:** Charles Murray and the New Right see the underclass as the undeserving poor who have different values and behaviour from other people. Members of the underclass depend on welfare state benefits for their income and are unwilling to work in paid employment. **[Maximum 3 marks]**

Power and Authority

7. **Suggested answer:** Max Weber argued that power could be based on charismatic authority. People obey or support individuals with charismatic authority (such as Mahatma Gandhi or Nelson Mandela) because they have extraordinary personal qualities that inspire them. **[Maximum 3 marks]**

Power and the State

8. **Example answer:** Qualitative data. **[1]** The observer could gather rich qualitative data on a high-profile protest movement in the UK by covertly observing protests as they unfold and focusing on the way people interact and organise themselves. This would give the observer a detailed insight into the organisation of a protest. **[3] Other possible advantages:** Validity; if observation is covert, there will be no observer effect; it might be impossible to use other methods to obtain data if the protest movement engages in illegal activity – **1 mark for a relevant advantage and 3 marks for explaining this advantage.**

1. C
2. **Example answer:** Confidentiality. **[1]** I would keep all personal details and other research data concerning the parents and teenagers confidential so that a parent does not find out what their teenage son or daughter said about them during the research (or vice versa). Data would need to be anonymised and stored securely so that only authorised people could access it. **[3] Other possible ethical issues:** Anonymity; informed consent; avoiding harm to participants – **1 mark for a relevant ethical issue and 3 marks for explaining how you would deal with this issue.**

3. **Possible content: up to 4 marks for AO1; up to 4 marks for AO2; up to 4 marks for AO3.**
    *   Define the terms conjugal roles and feminism.
    *   Argue that conjugal roles have become joint rather than segregated; discuss Young and Willmott's symmetrical family study.
    *   Argue that changes in conjugal roles are due to feminism (e.g. feminism has influenced women's attitudes to paid employment and led them to reject the traditional housewife role). Feminism has also helped to bring about changes in employment laws and equal opportunities policies at work which impact on conjugal roles.
    *   Argue that the changes are due to other factors such as more effective contraception; women's increased financial independence; technological developments leading to more home-based leisure opportunities.
    *   Argue that conjugal roles have changed to a limited extent, e.g. women's dual burden and triple shift.
    *   Draw on Oakley's feminist criticisms of studies such as that of Young and Willmott.
    *   Reach a balanced conclusion that addresses 'how far'.

4. C
5. **Example answer:** Interviewer bias. **[1]** The issue of racism in higher education is potentially sensitive and the interviewer might influence the interviewee's responses. Interviewees might be influenced by the interviewer's style of interviewing, ethnicity, appearance or accent, and might not answer honestly, which would affect validity. They might underplay incidents of racism they have experienced in higher education. **[3] Other possible disadvantages:** Small sample size; sample unlikely to be representative; expensive given the amount of data collected; time-consuming compared with surveys; cannot be replicated to check reliability; cannot generalise – **1 mark for a relevant disadvantage and 3 marks for explaining this disadvantage.**

6. **Possible content: up to 4 marks for AO1; up to 4 marks for AO2; up to 4 marks for AO3.**
    *   Outline the differences in educational achievements linked to social class, ethnicity and gender.
    *   Argue that school-based factors are the most important issue by discussing school processes such as teacher expectations of girls and boys, students from working-class and minority ethnic backgrounds; labelling and the self-fulfilling prophecy; the possible effects of banding and streaming; the gendered curriculum; the ethnocentric curriculum; school-based resources; school ethos; institutional racism.
    *   Argue that student cultures and peer pressure inside and outside school are the most important factor.
    *   Argue that home-based factors are more important than school-based factors in explaining different achievements by discussing parental values and expectations; material deprivation; cultural capital.
    *   Argue that government funding and policies such as marketisation and equal opportunities legislation are more important.
    *   Reach a balanced conclusion that addresses 'how far'.

7. C
8. **Example answer:** Observing and getting drawn into criminal activity. **[1]** To gain the acceptance and trust of the criminal sub-culture's members, the researcher might get drawn into illegal activity and end up breaking the law, getting arrested and prosecuted. If they have a criminal conviction, this could affect their reputation and career. **[3] Other possible disadvantages:** Ethical dilemmas if the researcher observes a crime; arousing hostility among the sub-cultures' members; practical disadvantages of time and cost; over-involvement leading to bias; the observer effect could result in invalid findings – **1 mark for a relevant disadvantage and 3 marks for explaining this disadvantage.**

9. **Possible content: up to 4 marks for AO1; up to 4 marks for AO2; up to 4 marks for AO3.**
    *   Define the terms deviance and peer pressure.
    *   Argue that peer pressure is the most important factor in explaining anti-social behaviour among young people.
    *   Argue that the main reason is status frustration leading to membership of a delinquent sub-culture.

- Argue that home-based factors are more important, e.g. inadequate socialisation; the values of the underclass.
- Argue that anomie is the most important factor.
- Argue that structural factors are most important: Marxists argue that the criminal justice system is biased against working-class and black youth.
- Reach a balanced conclusion that addresses 'how far'.

10. **A**

11. **Example answer:** One disadvantage is the difficulty in maintaining contact with the original sample over time. **[1]** To study social mobility, a sociologist must keep track of the occupations of the sample group over the years, or even decades. However, it is difficult to keep in contact with the sample when people change their phone number, move house or move abroad. People in the sample may not feel the need to inform the researcher when they move. Over time, the sample could become less representative of the population. **[3] Other possible disadvantages:** People withdrawing from the study; the timescale means that they are expensive – **1 mark for a relevant disadvantage and 3 marks for explaining this disadvantage.**

12. **Possible content: up to 4 marks for AO1; up to 4 marks for AO2; up to 4 marks for AO3.**
- Define the term poverty.
- Argue that the behaviour of individuals and families is the most important reason by discussing the culture of poverty and the cycle of deprivation.
- Argue that people's behaviour is the most important reason by discussing New Right ideas about the underclass and welfare dependency.
- Argue that structural factors are more important than individual factors by discussing Marxist accounts of poverty as linked to class-based inequalities in capitalist society.
- Argue that structural factors are more important by discussing feminist accounts of poverty as linked to gender-based inequalities such as the gender pay gap.
- Argue that structural factors such as the impact of unemployment, globalisation and inadequacies of the welfare state are most important.
- Reach a balanced conclusion that addresses 'how far'.

Glossary

Absolute poverty – people in absolute poverty have incomes that are insufficient to obtain the minimum needed to survive, such as food or shelter.

Academies – schools that have left local authority control and whose funding is provided directly by government. All schools have been encouraged to convert to academy status since 2010.

Achieved status – social positions that are earned on the basis of personal talents or merit.

Achievement – academic performance or attainment within education.

Adolescence: the period of time in an individual's life between childhood and adulthood.

Affluence – having a lot of money and material possessions.

Ageing population – in an ageing population, the proportion of the population over retirement age is gradually increasing.

Ageism – discrimination based on age.

Agencies of formal social control – agencies of the state such as the police force, the courts and prisons that exercise control over people's behaviour based on written laws and rules.

Agencies of informal social control – groups and organisations such as workmates, peer groups, families and religions that control people's behaviour based on social processes such as approval and disapproval.

Agencies of primary socialisation – groups in society such as families that are responsible for early childhood learning and socialisation.

Agencies of secondary socialisation – groups and organisations such as peer groups, religions and the mass media through which people learn society's norms and values.

Agencies (or agents) of social control – the groups and organisations in society that control or constrain people's behaviour and actions.

Agency (or agent) of socialisation – a social group or institution responsible for undertaking socialisation, such as a family, peer group, school, workplace, religion and the mass media.

Agenda setting – the ability of the media to focus public attention on particular topics and thereby direct public discussion and debate onto these topics.

Alienation – under capitalism, the workers feel estranged or cut off from their work because they have no control over production or the products of their labour.

Anomie – a situation of normlessness in which the norms that regulate people's behaviour break down.

Anti-school sub-culture – a school-based group of students who resist the school, its teachers and their authority, and openly challenge the school rules.

Anti-social behaviour – behaviour that causes harassment, distress or alarm to other people.

Aristocracy – a class of privileged people who have hereditary titles such as Duke or Lady and who are usually wealthy landowners.

Arranged marriage – a marriage in which the family or relatives of the prospective spouses take the leading role in finding a suitable partner for them. However, the prospective spouses have the right to choose whether to accept the arrangement.

Ascribed status – social positions that are fixed at birth and unchanging over time, including a hereditary title linked to family background (Princess or Lord, for example).

Assimilation – the process by which immigrants abandon their own culture and adapt their behaviour to fit the norms and values of the dominant culture. (See also multiculturalism.)

Asylum seekers – people who have left their country of origin and moved to another country in order to seek protection from persecution.

Attitude survey – a social survey that measures respondents' views and thoughts on particular issues.

Authority – the exercise of power based on consent or agreement.

Benefit cheats – people who claim welfare state benefits that they are not entitled to.

Bias – being one-sided rather than neutral or open-minded. Bias can operate either in favour of or against an idea, group or point of view.

Bigamy – the offence of getting married to someone while already married to someone else.

Blended (or reconstituted) family – a family in which one or both partners have a child or children from a previous relationship.

Bourgeois – relating to or belonging to the bourgeoisie.

Bourgeoisie – the ruling class who own the means of production (for example, the factories, big businesses or land) and exploit the proletariat in order to make huge profits.

Bureaucracy – an organisation (such as a government department) that operates as a hierarchy with a clear set of rules.

Bureaucratic authority – authority based on a set of rules that operate within a bureaucracy.

Canalisation – the way parents channel their children's interests into toys, games and other activities that are seen as gender appropriate.

Capitalism – an economic system that generates extreme wealth for the bourgeoisie.

Capitalist – can refer to capitalism as an economic system; can also refer to members of the bourgeoisie (the capitalists who form the ruling class).

Case study – a detailed study of a particular institution (such as a school or hospital) or a series of related events (such as the moral panic surrounding mods and rockers).

Caste – an example of a stratification system linked to Hinduism and operating in India. People are born into a particular caste or strata and their social position is ascribed at birth.

Censorship – the control of information and ideas in a society, often via governmental control of the press, television and other means of communication.

Census – a questionnaire survey conducted every 10 years in the UK to collect information on the whole population.

Changing social attitudes – changes in people's views and opinions on social issues such as divorce or cohabitation.

Charismatic authority – obedience based on a person's charisma or exceptional personal qualities.

Childhood – the period of time in a person's life between birth and becoming an adult. The term 'child' usually refers to younger children.

Child-rearing – bringing up children.

Chivalry thesis – the idea that the criminal justice system treats female offenders, particularly those who conform to gender stereotypes, more leniently than male offenders.

Citizenship – a political and legal status linked to membership of a particular state.

Class alignment – strong links between class and voting behaviour with working-class people voting Labour and middle-class people voting Conservative.

Class deal – a 'deal' that offers women material rewards such as consumer goods in return for working for a wage.

Class dealignment – weakening of the links between social class and voting behaviour.

Class struggle – in capitalist society, class conflict occurs between the bourgeoisie (the owners of the means of production) and the proletariat (the working class), who have competing interests.

Classless society – a society in which there is no private ownership of property and so no clearly structured social classes.

Closed question – a fixed-choice question that requires the respondent to choose between a number of given answers.

Cohabitation – living with a partner outside marriage or civil partnership.

Commune – a group of people who live together and share possessions, wealth and property. Communes may be based, for example, on shared political beliefs or environmental principles.

Communism – a system involving communal ownership rather than individual ownership of private property.

Community – a particular area and its residents (e.g. the local community) or a group of people who share a sense of identity (e.g. Manchester's Irish community).

Community service – a sentence that involves an offender having to do unpaid work in the community. The term is also sometimes used to refer to unpaid voluntary work, such as helping out in a charity shop.

Competition – a struggle or contest between individuals or groups to obtain something desirable (such as qualifications, school places, status, power or wealth) that is in limited supply.

Comprehensive school – a non-selective secondary school that admits all children regardless of their ability.

Confidentiality – an agreement that all information (for example, from research participants) will only be accessed by those who have the authority to access it.

Conformity – behaviour that complies with or follows society's norms and values.

Conjugal relationship – the relationship between a married or cohabiting couple.

Conjugal roles – the domestic roles of married or cohabiting partners.

Consensus – broad agreement on norms and values.

Constituency – a specific area in which the constituents elect an MP to represent them in Parliament.

Content analysis – the analysis of documents and images (e.g. media products) by constructing a set of categories, coding sections of the content according to these categories, and then counting the number of times a theme appears.

Continuity – lack of social change; social structures, values, norms, attitudes, behaviour and so on remain the same over time.

Control theory – an approach that focuses on why most people conform. People are seen as behaving rationally and they are controlled through a deal that offers them rewards for conforming. They are likely to conform when they think the rewards are worth it.

Conventional family – a traditional nuclear family containing a married couple and their children who live together.

Corporate crime – crimes committed by employees on behalf of the company or organisation they work for. Examples include the manufacture and sale of unsafe products.

Correspondence principle – the way in which what is learned in school through the hidden curriculum mirrors what is required when in the workplace. For example, how schools are organised and how control is exerted will mirror that of the workplace in a capitalist society.

Counter-school culture – a group within a school that rejects the values and norms of the school and replaces them with anti-school values and norms.

Covert observation – a researcher observes a group in order to study it but without informing its members about his or her research activities.

Crime – an illegal act (such as shoplifting or murder) that is punishable by law.

Crime rate – a measure of crime in terms of the number of incidents of a particular crime per specified number of adults over a given period. For example, six robberies per 1000 adults in a particular year.

Criminality – criminal acts; involvement in behaviour that breaks the criminal law.

Criminal justice system – the various agencies involved in law enforcement such as the police, the courts, the prison service and the probation service.

Criminal subculture – a social group whose members' values and behaviour involve breaking the law.

Crisis of masculinity – the idea that males see their traditional masculine identity as under threat today. For example, they no longer have a clear-cut role in society.

Cross-cultural studies – studies that explore similarities and differences between societies or cultures.

Cultural capital – the knowledge, attitudes and values that the middle class provide for their children that gives them an advantage in the education system.

Cultural deprivation – a theory that suggests that some working-class and minority ethnic students lack the 'correct' values, behaviours and attitudes from socialisation to succeed in education.

Cultural diversity – culturally based differences between people in a society in terms of religion, ethnicity, social class, etc.

Cultural values – the values of a particular culture. (See values.)

Culture – the whole way of life of a particular society or social group. Culture includes the values, norms, customs, beliefs, knowledge, skills and language of the group or society.

Culture of dependency – a way of life that is centred on reliance on welfare benefits.

Curriculum – the subject content taught in a school.

Cycle of deprivation – the idea that deprivation and poverty are passed on from parents to their children.

Dark figure of crime – hidden or invisible crimes (such as unreported and unrecorded crimes) that are not included within official statistics on crimes.

Data – information collected and analysed during the research process.

Data analysis – interpreting or making sense of the information collected during research and summarising the main findings or results.

Data protection – research participants who are identifiable within the data held by researchers have legal protection and, for example, can ask to see this data.

Deferential – behaving in a way that shows respect to someone such as an elder or superior.

Delinquency – minor crime and deviance, usually committed by young people.

Democracy – government by the people.

Dependent family members – family members who depend on others within the family due to their age, for example, or lack of money. Dependent children, for instance, are those aged 0 to 15 or those aged 16 to 18 in full-time education and living with their parents.

Deschooling – the idea that the education system as it is currently organised should be abolished.

Deviance – behaviour that does not conform to society's norms and values and, if detected, is likely to lead to negative sanctions. Deviance can be – but is not necessarily – illegal.

Deviancy amplification – the process whereby public and media reaction to deviance leads to an increase in – or amplifies – deviance by provoking more of the same behaviour.

Deviant career – the process by which individuals come to see themselves as deviant and, possibly, join a deviant subculture.

Dictatorship – political power is concentrated in the hands of an individual ruler who rules by force.

Direct action – a campaign to raise awareness on an issue such as climate change or tax avoidance. Tactics include occupying buildings such as shops or banks.

Discrimination – less favourable or unfair treatment based, for example, on an individual's gender, ethnicity or age.

Distribution (of power and of wealth) – the way in which power and wealth are shared out among different groups in society.

Division of domestic labour – see domestic division of labour.

Divorce – the legal termination (or ending) of a marriage.

Domestic division of labour – the division of tasks such as housework, childcare and DIY between men and women within the home.

Double deviance thesis – the idea that female offenders are treated more harshly than male offenders within the criminal justice system because their offending behaviour is seen not just as illegal but also as unfeminine.

Double shift – many married or cohabiting women work two shifts by doing a paid job and also most of the housework and caring for the family. This is sometimes referred to as the dual burden.

Double standard – a rule or code of behaviour that is unfairly applied to one group (such as women) and not another (such as men). For example, norms surrounding sexual behaviour allow young men more freedom than young women.

Dual-career family – a family in which two adults have careers.

Dysfunctional family – a family in which functions such as providing emotional support are not being carried out. Dysfunctional families are characterised by social problems such as domestic violence or child abuse.

Economic function (of families) – from a functionalist approach, this is the function that the family carries out by providing its members with financial support, food and shelter. From a Marxist approach, the family has an economic function under capitalism because women, as housewives and mothers, carry out unpaid domestic labour (such as child-rearing, cleaning and cooking) that benefits the capitalist system.

Economy – a system by which goods and services are produced, distributed and consumed in a region or country. Examples include capitalism and socialism.

Education – the process of teaching and learning that takes place in schools, colleges, etc.

Educational reform – changes to the education system.

Egalitarian – based on the idea that people are equal.

Eleven plus – a national IQ test introduced by the 1944 Education Act to be used as a method of allocating students to one of three types of school in the tripartite system.

Elite – a group that has the most power in a society based on its wealth or privilege.

Embourgeoisement thesis – a hypothesis suggesting that working-class families are becoming middle class in their norms and values as their incomes and standards of living improve.

Emigration – the act of leaving one country to live in another.

Empty nest family – a family containing a mature couple who live together after their children have left home.

Empty shell marriage – a marriage in which the couple continue to live together (for example, for the sake of their children) even though the marriage has broken down.

Environmental poverty – a way of measuring deprivation in terms of conditions such as inadequate housing, lack of a garden, inadequate outdoor play facilities and air pollution.

Established or state church – the Church of England is the established church in England. It is linked to the state and the monarch is its Supreme Governor.

Ethical considerations – issues such as informed consent and confidentiality that sociologists must consider in order to conduct morally acceptable research.

Ethnic diversity – having a range of different ethnic groups in a society.

Ethnic group – a social group whose members share an identity based on their cultural traditions or cultural characteristics such as religion or language. Britain is home to a wide range of minority ethnic groups, including those of Irish, Polish, Greek Cypriot, Indian and African Caribbean heritage.

Ethnic minority – a group in a particular society that has different cultural traditions from the ethnic majority.

Ethnicity – cultural traditions, norms and values that distinguish the members of a particular social group from other groups.

Ethnocentric curriculum – the curriculum is seen as judging things in a biased way from the point of view of one culture. For example, the National Curriculum may value white, Western literature, art, history, etc.

Ethnography – the study of people's culture and practices in everyday settings, usually based on qualitative methods such as participant observation and unstructured interviews.

Ethos (of school) – the distinctive character and values of a particular school.

Exclusion (from school) – the temporary or permanent removal of a student from a school.

Expectations – hopes or beliefs, for example about what marriage will – or should – be like.

Expressive role – the caring, emotional and nurturing role in the family. Parsons sees this as the woman's natural role in the family.

Extended family – a group of relatives extending beyond the nuclear family. The classic extended family contains three generations who either live under the same roof or nearby. This type of extension is known as vertical extension. In horizontally extended families, two generations live together or nearby. In modified extended families, members live apart geographically but maintain regular contact and provide support.

False class consciousness – subordinate groups such as the proletariat suffer from false consciousness when they do not recognise that they are being exploited or their true interests.

Family – an important social structure that can be broadly defined as a couple whose relationship is based on marriage, civil partnership or cohabitation, with or without dependent children, or a lone parent and their child or children.

Family diversity – the different types of family such as nuclear and lone-parent families. Aspects of family diversity also include social class, culture and cohort.

Fascism – a political movement that began with Mussolini, a dictator who came to power in Italy in 1922. The term is now often used to describe right wing political ideas or a right wing political system based on racism and nationalism.

Fee paying school – a private or independent school that charges school fees.

Feminism – a sociological approach that examines the ways gender operates within social structures such as families and in the wider society. Feminists want equality in the power and status of women and men in society. Some see society as patriarchal.

Feminist – a sociologist who explores how gender operates in society and wants gender equality.

Feudalism – a stratification system in medieval Europe with the king at the top, then the lords, the knights and the peasants at the bottom.

First-past-the-post – an electoral system based on winner takes all. The candidate with the highest number of votes wins the seat.

Focus group – a type of group interview that focuses on one particular topic. It explores how people interact within the group and how they respond to each other's views.

Folk devil – a group that is defined as a threat to society's values and treated as a scapegoat.

Formal curriculum – the subjects taught and learning that takes place during timetabled lessons at school.

Formal education – education that takes place in educational establishments such as schools and universities where people learn knowledge and skills across a wide range of subjects.

Formal social control – constraints on people's behaviour based on written laws and rules. It is usually associated with the ways that the state regulates and controls behaviour. (See also agencies of formal social control.)

Free schools – schools that are funded directly by the state but are set up and run by parents, teachers, businesses and faith groups.

Functionalism – a sociological approach that examines society's structures (such as the family, the education system and religion) in terms of the functions they perform for the continuation of society and for individuals.

Functionally important roles – key positions in society that, for example, provide essential services and ensure society's survival over time.

Fundamentalism – belief in the literal interpretation of religious scriptures.

Further education (FE) – this sector mainly caters for students aged 16 years and over. Courses are usually provided by sixth form and FE colleges.

Gatekeepers – the media professionals (programme controllers, editors and journalists) and owners who decide what gets covered and how it is edited and presented.

Gender – relates to socially constructed or cultural (rather than biological) differences between men and women that are associated with masculinity and femininity.

Gender deal – a 'deal' that offers women emotional and material rewards in return for living with a male breadwinner within a family.

Gender equality – men and women have the same opportunities and rights in society, for example in relation to education and employment.

Gender roles – the behaviour expected of people based on their gender and associated with masculinity and femininity.

Gendered curriculum – a curriculum in which some subjects (including high status subjects such as maths and science) are associated with masculinity and others (such as languages and humanities) are associated with femininity.

Geographical mobility – moving house from one area to live in another area, region or town.

Glass ceiling – an invisible barrier to promotion at work faced by some groups including women.

Globalisation – the process by which societies, cultures and economies become increasingly interconnected.

Hidden curriculum – things learned indirectly in school that are not formally taught, such as valuing punctuality or conformity and obedience.

Higher education (HE) – this sector includes universities that provide higher level academic and vocational courses (such as degrees).

Home tuition – teaching children at home rather than at school, usually by parents or private tutors.

Hypothesis – a supposition, hunch or informed guess, usually written as a statement that can be tested and then either supported by the evidence or proved wrong.

Idealisation – the representation of the traditional nuclear family as the ideal type of family.

Identity – how we see ourselves (our self-identity) and how others see us. Sources of identity include our gender, age, ethnicity, social class, religion and sexuality. 'Identity' can also refer to a person's personal details such as their name and address.

Identity theft – a crime in which the perpetrator gets hold of, or steals, personal information from a victim and uses it for personal gain.

Image – a representation or picture of a particular social group as presented, for example, in the mass media. Media images of some groups are often distorted.

Immigrant – a person who has migrated to another country in order to live and work there.

Immigration – the process of moving to another country in order to live and work there.

Income – the flow of resources that individuals and households receive over a specific period of time. Income may be received in cash (for example from earnings) or in kind (for instance a petrol allowance).

Independent schools – fee-paying private and public schools that are independent of the state sector.

Indictable offence – a serious criminal offence such as murder and robbery that is tried in the Crown Court before a judge and jury.

Industrial dispute – a disagreement or conflict between employers and employees over issues such as hours, pay and work conditions.

Informal education – learning that takes place when people develop knowledge and skills by observing what is happening around them in everyday life.

Informal social control – constraints on people's behaviour based on social processes such as the approval and disapproval of others. Informal social control is enforced via social pressure. (See also agencies of informal social control.)

Informed consent – before carrying out research, sociologists must obtain permission from potential research participants. Giving informed consent means that a research participant only agrees to take part in the research once the sociologist has explained fully what the research is about and why it is being carried out.

Institutional racism – this occurs when an organisation (such as a police force or hospital) fails to provide an appropriate service to people because of their ethnic origin, culture or colour. Institutional racism can be seen in organisational attitudes or behaviour that discriminates, even when individuals themselves act without intending this.

Instrumental role – the breadwinner role in the family. Parsons sees this as the male's role in the family.

Instrumentalism – an attitude or approach to something (such as paid work) where it is a means to an end (e.g. the wages provide a comfortable lifestyle) rather than an end in itself (e.g. job satisfaction).

Integrated conjugal roles – roles that are shared equally between married or cohabiting partners.

Intelligence quotient (IQ) – a score based on a test designed to measure a person's intelligence.

Interactionism – a perspective that focuses on how people interact on a daily basis. Interactionists describe social reality by interpreting the feelings and actions of the people involved.

Interest group – see **pressure group**.

Inter-generational – between the generations.

Interpretivism – an approach in sociology that tries to understand people's lived experiences and the meanings they attach to their behaviour.

Interview – a method used to collect data in a study. In general, the interviewer asks questions and the interviewee responds.

Isolation – the idea that the nuclear family has become more detached or separated from the wider family.

Joint conjugal roles – domestic roles that are divided or shared in an equal way between married or cohabiting partners.

Judiciary – judges and magistrates (or Justices of the Peace – JPs – as they are also known) who sit in courts and apply the law.

Kibbutz – a group of people who live communally in settlements in Israel and who value equality and cooperation between kibbutz members.

Kibbutzim – plural of kibbutz.

Kin – relatives.

Kinship – links between people based on ties of blood, marriage or adoption.

Labelling – the process of attaching a label (a sticky tag), characteristic or definition to individuals or groups.

Law – a formal rule, usually passed by the government and enforced by the state, that regulates people's behaviour.

League tables – tables of school and college results published annually to allow parents and others to make comparisons based on achievement levels.

Left and right wing – terms used to describe political parties, ideas and movements. The left wing includes socialists and communists while the right wing includes conservatives and fascists.

Legal rational authority – see rational legal authority.

Legislation – this can refer to a law or a set of laws that the government makes; it can also refer to the process of making laws.

Legislative process – the process of making laws.

Legislature – the body in a country or state that has the authority to make or change the laws. In the UK, for example, Parliament has authority to make laws.

Liberal democratic values – a set of values (such as valuing freedom of speech, movement and information) associated with representative democracies.

Life chances – an individual's chances of achieving positive or negative outcomes (relating, for example, to health, education, housing) as they progress through life.

Life expectancy – the average number of years a person can expect to live.

Lifestyles – the way in which people live, including their leisure and work patterns. Lifestyle is influenced by factors such as religion, age, income and social class.

Lone-parent family – a family consisting of one parent and a child or children who live together.

Longitudinal study – a study of the same group of people conducted over a period of time. After the initial survey or interview has taken place, follow-up surveys or interviews are carried out at intervals over a number of years.

Lumpenproletariat – a social class made up of the 'drop-outs' and criminals of society.

Magistrates – volunteers (JPs) who sit in the Magistrates' Court and deal with less serious crime.

Male domination – the exercise of power and control by men over women in society.

Market situation – people's position (e.g. their skills) in relation to the labour market. Weber saw class situation in terms of market situation.

Marketisation (of education) – the policy of bringing market forces (such as competition and choice) into education.

Marriage – the legal union between two people.

Marxism – a sociological approach that draws on the ideas of Karl Marx and applies them to modern capitalist societies.

Marxist – sociologists who draw on the ideas of Karl Marx and apply them to contemporary capitalist societies.

Mass media – forms of communication (media) that reach large (mass) audiences, including newspapers, magazines, books, television, cinema and the internet.

Master status – a status such as 'junkie' or 'thief' that becomes a dominant status and overrides all of an individual's other statuses such as daughter, sister, friend or employee.

Matriarch – a woman who holds power and authority.

Matriarchal family – a family in which a woman holds power and authority.

Means of production – the raw materials and tools used in the production process. Under capitalism, these include property, factories and machinery.

Means testing – a means test is used to establish that a claimant is in financial need before they receive financial help from the state.

Media amplification – media exaggeration of the significance of a social issue or problem by over-reporting it.

Member of Parliament (MP) – a politician who has been elected to represent their constituents in the House of Commons.

Meritocracy – a system in which individuals' achievements are based on their own talents and efforts rather than their social origins and backgrounds.

Middle class – a social class made up of people who work in non-manual, managerial and professional occupations.

Migration – the movement of people either nationally, from one region of a country to another, or internationally from one country to another.

Miscarriage of justice – this occurs when a court fails to administer justice by, for example, finding an innocent person guilty of a crime.

Mixed ability – where children are taught in classes that are not organised based on ability or through setting or streaming.

Mixed methods research – the use of different methods within one project to generate both quantitative and qualitative data.

Monarchy – a system with a Queen or King as the head of state.

Monogamy – the practice of being married to only one person at a time.

Moral panic – a media-fuelled over-reaction to social groups (such as 'hoodies'). This process involves the media exaggerating the extent and significance of a social problem. A particular group is cast as a folk devil and becomes defined as a threat to society's values.

Multiculturalism – the view that the cultural differences between, and identities of, the various groups in a culturally diverse society should be respected and maintained. (See also assimilation.)

National curriculum – the subject content to be taught in state schools as decided by government.

Neoconservatism – a political perspective linked to the New Right that believes in traditional values and aims to change the moral and cultural fabric of society.

Neoliberalism – a political perspective linked to the New Right that believes competition, choice and privatisation are the most effective ways to run aspects of society. For example, parents and students are seen as consumers within the education sector.

New man – a caring, sharing man who rejects sexist attitudes, believes in gender equality and puts this into practice by, for example, sharing domestic tasks and childcare.

New Right – a political perspective associated with Charles Murray. It believes that the influence of the state in society should be reduced and that the market should have more of a role, e.g. the marketisation of education. It also stresses the importance of traditional values such as self-reliance rather than relying on the welfare state.

New social movements – loosely organised groups that aim to bring about social change. Examples include animal rights, environmental and gay rights groups. Many are global rather than national movements.

News values – media professionals' ideas about what issues and personalities are seen as newsworthy, topical or important.

Non-indictable offence – a less serious crime such as damage to property that is tried in a magistrates' court rather than a Crown Court.

Non-participant observation – a research method in which a sociologist observes the community or group being studied but does not take part in any of its activities.

Norms – the rules that define appropriate and expected behaviour in particular social settings, such as in cinemas or aeroplanes.

Nuclear family – a family containing a father, mother and their child or children. It contains two generations and family members live together in the same household. The parents may be married or cohabiting outside marriage.

Observation – a research method in which a sociologist gathers data by observing the community or group being studied.

Official crime statistics – existing sources of quantitative data on crime compiled, for example, by government departments such as the Home Office.

Ofsted – the Office for Standards in Education, Children's Services and Skills; a government department.

Oligarchy – a small group of powerful individuals who control an organisation or a country usually to further their own interests.

Open-ended question – a question that allows respondents to put forward their own answers rather than choose a response from several pre-set answers.

Participant observation – a qualitative research method in which the researcher joins a group and takes part in its daily activities in order to study it.

Particularistic standards – in the family, children are judged against the standards and rules of their particular family and its values.

Patriarchal family – families in which men hold power and authority.

Patriarchy – male power, authority and dominance over women.

Petty bourgeoisie – a social class made up of owners of small businesses.

Pluralism – an approach which argues that a range of views, interests and opinions exists in society and no one group dominates the political process.

Police caution – a warning given to someone who has committed a minor crime such as graffiti.

Political party – an organisation such as the Labour or Conservative Party that has policies on a range of issues (such as education and crime), seeks to win an election and form a government.

Political socialisation – the process by which people acquire their political beliefs, values and preferences. Agencies include the media, families and workplaces.

Polyandry – a type of polygamy in which a woman has more than one husband at the same time.

Polygamy – a form of marriage in which an individual has more than one husband or wife at the same time.

Polygyny – a type of polygamy in which a man has more than one wife at the same time.

Popular press – the daily tabloid newspapers or 'red tops' that get large readerships.

Population – the particular group under study from which the sample is selected. The population may consist of people such as higher education students or institutions such as schools depending on the aims of the research.

Positivism – an approach that argues that the methods of the natural sciences should be used to study society. This approach focuses on how society influences human behaviour.

Poverty – there are two broad approaches to defining poverty: absolute poverty and relative poverty. (See **absolute poverty; relative poverty**.)

Poverty trap – people can be trapped in poverty if an increase in income reduces the benefits they are entitled to. For example, an employed person receiving means-tested benefits could be worse off after a wage rise if they now earn too much to qualify for benefits.

Power – in social relationships between individuals (for example, between spouses or parents and children) or groups, power usually refers to the dominance and control of one individual or group over others.

Prejudice – a prejudgement in favour of, or against, a person, group or issue. Prejudice involves opinions and beliefs rather than action.

Pressure group – a group of people who share an interest and try to persuade the government to adopt a particular policy or to influence public opinion on an issue.

Primary data – information that is generated and collected at first hand by doing research using techniques such as questionnaires, interviews or observation.

Primary socialisation – the process of early childhood learning, usually in families, during which babies and children acquire the basic behaviour patterns, language and skills they need in later life.

Prime Minister – a politician who is head of the UK government.

Principle of stratified diffusion – the idea that social changes start at the top of the social stratification system and spread downwards. Changes in family life, for instance, spread from the middle class into the working class.

Prison service – a part of the criminal justice system that detains convicted offenders who have been given a prison sentence.

Private schools – fee-paying schools that are independent of the state sector.

Privatised instrumentalism – social relationships centred on the home rather than work. Paid work is a means to an end.

Privatised nuclear family – a nuclear family that is cut off from the extended family. The lifestyle tends to focus on the home.

Probation service – a part of the criminal justice system that is responsible for supervising high-risk offenders who have been released into the community.

Proletarianisation – the idea that clerical workers have experienced downward mobility into the working class. Their work has become less skilled and more routine, and now resembles factory work.

Proletariat – wage labourers who do not own any means of production and live by selling their labour to the bourgeoisie for wages.

Propaganda – information (often biased or false) that is used to promote, for example, a particular viewpoint, cause or government.

Proportional representation (PR) – under a PR electoral system, seats are allocated according to the total number of votes that each party receives.

Protest movement – an organised effort to create social or political change. Tactics include demonstrations, gatherings and marches, possibly in many cities across the world at once.

Public examinations – examinations (such as GCSEs and A Levels) that are set by an exam board such as AQA or OCR.

Public schools – the older and more famous independent schools, such as Eton and Harrow.

Qualitative data – information presented as words or quotations rather than numbers.

Quality press – newspapers that cover serious news issues such as UK politics, world news, the global economy and business.

Quantitative data – information presented in numerical form, for example as graphs, bar charts, pie charts or tables of statistics.

Questionnaire – a set of structured, standardised questions delivered to respondents.

Quota sampling – a sampling technique in which an interviewer must question an exact quota (number) of people from categories such as females or teenagers, in proportion to their numbers in the wider population.

Racial discrimination – see racism.

Racism – racism or racial discrimination occurs when people are treated differently and less favourably on the basis of their ethnicity.

Random sample – a sample (subgroup) in which each member of the population has a known chance of being selected for inclusion in the sample.

Rational legal authority – a type of authority in which obedience is based on the operation of a set of rules or laws.

Reconstituted (or blended) family – a family in which one or both partners have a child or children from a previous relationship.

Recorded crime – crime that is recorded by the police and appears in police-recorded crime statistics.

Relative deprivation – lacking material resources compared to other people in society.

Relative income standard of poverty – a measure of poverty based on how much income a household has compared to other households. One way, for example, would be to put households in rank order according to their income and then identify 10 per cent of households with the lowest incomes.

Relative poverty – people in relative poverty cannot afford to meet the general standard of living of most other people in their society.

Reliability – refers to consistency. Research findings are reliable if, after the research is repeated a second time using the same methods, the same or consistent results are obtained the second time round.

Reported crime – crime that is reported to the police.

Representative sample – reflects the characteristics of its population. It is just like the population but a smaller version of it.

Research – the collection of data in an organised way by methods such as questionnaires or interviews.

Respondent – the person from whom information is sought.

Right of appeal – a person who is found guilty of a criminal offence may be granted the right to appeal against (or challenge) this verdict.

Role conflict – this occurs when the demands of one role (for example, student) conflict or clash with those of another (for example, friend or part-time employee).

Role – the pattern of expected and acceptable behaviour of people who occupy a particular status or social position. The role of 'teacher', for instance, defines how we expect a teacher to behave during the working day.

Ruling-class ideology – a set of dominant ideas in society that distort reality and serve the interests of the bourgeoisie.

Rural – relating to country (as opposed to urban) life. Rural areas are more sparsely populated than cities.

Same-sex family – a family in which a same-sex couple live together with their child or children.

Sample – a subgroup of the population selected for study.

Sampling frame – a complete list of all members of the population from which a sample is drawn. Examples include membership lists, school registers and the Royal Mail's list of postcode addresses.

Sanctions – rewards or punishments to those who conform to or break the rules.

SATs – standard assessment tests or national curriculum tests.

Scapegoat – an individual or a group that is blamed for something that is not their fault.

Secondary data – information that already exists and has previously been generated or collected by other people. Sources include official statistics, the mass media, autobiographies and studies by other sociologists.

Secondary socialisation – through this process, which begins during later childhood and continues throughout our adult lives, we learn society's norms and values. Agencies of secondary socialisation include peer groups, religions and the mass media.

Secularisation – the process whereby the influence of religion in a society declines.

Segregated conjugal roles – domestic roles of married or cohabiting partners which are separated out or divided in an unequal way.

Selective benefits – means-tested welfare benefits that are targeted at those in greatest financial need rather than available to everyone, regardless of income and savings.

Selective schools – schools that select their intake by having some form of entry requirement such as an entrance examination.

Self-fulfilling prophecy – this occurs when a person who has been labelled comes to fit the image people have of them; i.e. the prediction comes true.

Self-report study – a study that asks respondents whether they have committed particular offences during a specified time period such as the last year. It provides information on offenders and offences that are not necessarily dealt with by the police or courts.

Separate spheres (in relation to the role of women) – the split between the private world of home and the public world of work.

Serial monogamy – the practice of divorcing, remarrying, divorcing, remarrying, and so on.

Setting (in education) – where students are placed into ability groups for each specific subject.

Sex discrimination – treating someone differently and less favourably on the basis of their sex (or gender).

Sex equality – see gender equality.

Sexism – discrimination based on sex (or gender).

Slavery – a form of stratification in which one group claims the right to own another group and treat them as property.

Snowball sampling – a sampling technique in which the researcher contacts one member of the population and through them identifies others in the same population who then provide additional contacts.

Social change – an alteration in social structures, attitudes, behaviour, relationships, norms, values, and so on.

Social class – a form of social stratification based on economic factors such as occupation and income (how people earn a living).

Social cohesion – the idea that people in society should have a shared set of values and attitudes that help to unite society and to bring people together.

Social construct – a product of society or culture. Crime statistics are a social product in that they are the end product of a series of interactions, choices and decisions of the people involved.

Social control – control or constraints over people's actions and behaviour from society or groups. (See also **formal social control** and **informal social control**.)

Social conventions – the norms or accepted ways to behave in particular situations.

Social exclusion – being shut out or excluded from participation in society's social, economic, political and cultural life.

Social inequality – the uneven distribution of resources such as money and power, or of opportunities related to education and health.

Social issues – issues that affect groups, communities, societies and people's lives. Examples include the quality of parenting and care of the elderly.

Social mobility – movement up or down between the layers or strata of society. **Inter-generational social mobility** refers to movement up or down between the layers as measured between the generations of a family. **Intra-generational social mobility** refers to movement of an individual over the course of their life up or down from one occupational classification to another.

Social network – a network of relatives and friends.

Social order – occurs when society is stable, ordered and runs smoothly without continual disruption.

Social processes – processes in society that involve interaction between individuals, groups and social structures. The process of socialisation, for example, involves interaction between individuals and social structures such as families and education.

Social security – welfare state provision related to areas such as state pensions, benefits and healthcare.

Social stigma – the shame or disgrace attached to something. In the past, for example, having an illegitimate child (a child born outside marriage) was seen as a source of shame for women.

Social stratification – the way that society is structured or divided into hierarchical strata – or layers – with the most privileged at the top and the least favoured at the bottom. Social class is an example of a stratification system.

Social structures – the different 'parts' or institutions that make up society, such as families, education and stratification systems.

Social survey – research based on self-administered questionnaires or structured interviews. Questions are standardised so respondents answer an identical set of questions.

Socialisation – the process through which people learn the culture, norms and values of the group or society they were born into.

Socialism – a system in which capital, land, factories, etc. are not owned and controlled by a few private individuals but by the community as a whole.

Socially defined behaviour – behaviour (such as deviance) that is defined according to the social setting in which it occurs. What we consider as 'deviant behaviour', for example, does not depend on the behaviour or act itself but on the social setting and how others label it.

Society – a group of people who share a culture or a way of life.

Special school – a school dedicated to teaching children with special educational needs.

Specialist school – centres of excellence in particular subject areas, such as languages or technology. They were intended to raise standards of teaching and learning in these areas.

State standard of poverty – a measure of poverty based on the rates paid by the state, the level at which people are entitled to claim state benefits.

Status – can refer to social positions linked, for example, to occupations (such as teacher or train driver) and families (such as child or parent). It can also refer to the amount of prestige or social standing that members of a group or society give an individual in a particular social position.

Status frustration – feelings of anger or annoyance that people experience when denied the opportunity to get social status. Cohen argued that working-class boys experience this when they try but fail to meet middle-class expectations at school.

Step-parent – someone who is the social parent of their partner's child or children but not their biological parent.

Stereotype – a fixed, standardised, distorted and over-simplified view of the characteristics of particular groups such as women. Stereotypes are often based on prejudice.

Structural theory – a theory such as Marxism or functionalism that considers the structure and culture of society in its explanations rather than how people interact with each other.

Sub-culture – a social group that differs from the dominant or main culture in terms of its members' values, beliefs, customs, etc. Examples include travellers who have a nomadic way of life and youth sub-cultures such as Goths or Emos.

Subjective class – how people see or identify themselves in social class terms.

Subjective poverty – when people see themselves as being poor.

Surveillance – monitoring people and gathering information on them in order to prevent crime.

Surveys – see social surveys.

Symmetrical family – a family form in which spouses carry out different tasks but each makes a similar contribution within the home.

Systematic sampling – a sampling technique that involves taking every 'nth' item from the sampling frame, for example every tenth name from a college register to generate the required sample size.

Teacher expectations – assumptions that teachers make about students' future academic achievements based on their knowledge of students' current performance.

Technological change – developments in technology (such as computers, IVF and mobile phones).

Terrorism – the use of violence or intimidation in order to achieve a set of political aims.

Theoretical perspective – an approach such as functionalism, Marxism or feminism that provides a set of ideas to explain the social world.

Trade union – an organisation of employees or workers that protects and promotes its members' interests in the workplace.

Traditional authority – a type of authority in which obedience is based on custom and tradition.

Traditional family roles – conventional gender roles within the nuclear family such as the male breadwinner and female homemaker.

Trend – the general direction in which statistics on something (such as the divorce rate) move or change over time. For example, the divorce rate may increase or decrease over time.

Triangulation – cross checking the findings from a qualitative method against the findings from a quantitative method.

Tripartite system – created by the 1944 Education Act, this system used the 11-plus test to determine students' ability levels. Students were then allocated to one of three types of school based on their tested abilities (grammar, secondary modern or technical).

Underemployment – a situation in which workers are employed at less than full time, and are willing and available to work more hours than they currently do.

Underclass – a group whose norms and values are different from those of mainstream society, or people who experience long-term poverty and who are unable to earn a living.

Unemployment – a situation in which people do not have jobs but are actively seeking work and available to start work.

Universal benefits – welfare benefits that are available to everyone, regardless of their income and savings, rather than targeted at those in most financial need.

Universalistic standards – where people are judged by the standards of the wider society, which are applied in the same way to everyone. In school, each student is judged against the same standards, e.g. in terms of rules and exam criteria.

Unrepresentative sample – a sample (subgroup) that does not reflect the characteristics of its population.

Unstructured interviews – informal interviews that are like guided conversations based around a set of themes or points rather than a standardised interview schedule. The aim is to gather rich and detailed qualitative data.

Unwritten rules – informal or 'taken-for-granted' guidelines on how we are expected to behave in particular social settings.

Upper class – a social class made up of the rich and powerful, particularly those who have inherited wealth.

Urban – associated with cities.

Validity – findings are valid if they truly measure or capture what they are supposed to be studying.

Value consensus – broad agreement on values.

Values – beliefs and ideas about what is seen as desirable or worth striving for in a society. Values such as privacy and respect for life provide general guidelines for behaviour.

Victim survey – a survey that asks respondents about their experiences of crime, whether they have been victims of particular offences during a specified time period and, if so, whether they reported the crimes to the police.

Vocationalism in education: work or career-related education such as a Diploma in Health and Social Care or in Business and Administration.

Wage – a daily, weekly or monthly income that an employee earns from paid work.

Wealth – ownership of assets such as property, land and works of art as well as money held in savings accounts and shares in companies.

Welfare benefits – financial support such as Income Support provided by the state to help those in need.

Welfare reform – changes to the way the welfare system operates, for instance cutting or replacing state benefits.

Welfare scrounger – a negative term for people who are seen as taking advantage of welfare state benefits.

Welfare state – a system in which the state takes responsibility for protecting the health and welfare of its citizens and meeting their social needs. The state does this by providing services (for example, the NHS) and benefits (for example, Income Support).

White-collar crime – refers broadly to crimes committed by people in relatively high status positions, such as accountants, doctors or solicitors, during their work. Examples include tax evasion and 'fiddling' expense accounts at work.

White-collar work – clerical, administrative or managerial jobs.

Work–life balance – getting the priorities right between career (e.g. hours spent at the office, ambitions) and lifestyle (e.g. having time for family, leisure and health).

Working class – a social class made up of people engaged in manual occupations.

Worldview – a perspective on, or way of seeing, society and the social world.

Youth crime – criminal offences committed by young people.

Youth culture – a group of young people, such as emos and punks, who share a culture and style of dress which differs from that of older generations.

References

Ball, S.J. (1981) *Beachside Comprehensive. A Case Study of Secondary Schooling*, Cambridge: Cambridge University Press.

Ball, S.J., Bowe, R. and Gewirtz, S. (1994) 'Market forces and parental choice'. In: Tomlinson, S. (ed), *Education Reform and its Consequences*. London: IPPR/Rivers Oram Press.

Becker, H. (1963) *Outsiders: Studies in the Sociology of Deviance*. New York: Free Press of Glencoe.

Bowles, S. and Gintis, H. (1976) *Schooling in Capitalist America*, London: Routledge and Kegan Paul.

Carlen, P. (1988) *Women, Crime and Poverty*. Milton Keynes: Open University Press.

Cohen, A.K. (1955) *Delinquent Boys: The Culture of the Gang*. New York: Free Press.

Cohen, S. (1972) *Folk Devils and Moral Panics: The Creation of the Mods and Rockers*. London: MacGibbon and Kee.

Davis, K. and Moore, W.E. (1945) 'Some principles of stratification', *American Sociological Review*, 10 (2).

Delphy, C. and Leonard, D. (1992) *Familiar Exploitation: A New Analysis of Marriage in Contemporary Western Societies*. Cambridge: Polity Press.

Devine, F. (1992) *Affluent Workers Revisited: Privatism and the Working Class*. Edinburgh: Edinburgh University Press.

Goldthorpe, J.H. *et al.* (1969) *The Affluent Worker in the Class Structure*. Cambridge University Press.

Halsey, A.H., Heath, A.F. and Ridge, J.M. (1980) *Origins and Destinations*. Oxford: Clarendon Press.

Heidensohn, F. (1985) *Women and Crime*. Basingstoke: Macmillan Press Ltd.

Illich, I. (1995) *Deschooling Society*. London: Marion Boyars Publishers Ltd.

Merton, R.K. (1938) *Social Theory and Social Structure*, New York: The Free Press.

Murdock, G.P. *Social Structure*. New York: Macmillan.

Murray, C. (1984) *Losing Ground: American Social Policy, 1950–1980*. New York: Basic Books.

Murray, C. (1996) 'The emerging British underclass'. In: Lister, R. (ed), *Charles Murray and the Underclass: The Developing Debate*. London: IEA.

Oakley, A. (1974) *Sociology of Housework*. London: Robertson.

Oakley, A. (1982) 'Conventional families'. In: Rapoport, R.N., Fogarty, M.P. and Rapoport, R. (eds), *Families in Britain*. London: Routledge and Kegan Paul. pp. 123–137.

Office for National Statistics – see All couples/stepfamily (row 2): http://webarchive.nationalarchives.gov.uk/20160105160709/http://www.ons.gov.uk/ons/rel/family-demography/stepfamilies/2011/stepfamilies-rpt.html

Pahl, J. (1989) *Money and Marriage*. Basingstoke: Macmillan.

Parsons, T. (1961) 'The School class as a social system'. In: Halsey, A.H. *et al*, *Education, Economy and Society*. New York: The Free Press.

Parsons, T. (1956). In Parsons, T. and Bales, R.F. (eds) *Family, Socialization and Interaction Process.*

Rapoport, R. (eds) *Families in Britain*. London: Routledge and Kegan Paul. pp. 123–137.

Townsend, P. (1979) *Poverty in the United Kingdom*. London: Allen Lane and Penguin Books.

Walby, S. (1990) *Theorizing Patriarchy*. Oxford: Blackwell Publishers.

Weber, M. (1947) *The Theory of Social and Economic Organization*. New York: OUP.

Willis, P. (1977) *Learning to Labour*, Farnborough: Saxon House.

Young, M. and Willmott, P. (1957) *Family and Kinship in East London*. Routledge and Kegan Paul.

Young, M. and Willmott, P. (1973) *The Symmetrical Family*. Routledge and Kegan Paul.

Zaretsky, E. (1976) *Capitalism, the Family and Personal Life*. London: Pluto Press.

Index

Index

Notes

GCSE Sociology

Collins

AQA GCSE Revision
Sociology

Sociology

AQA
GCSE

Workbook

Pauline Wilson

Revision Tips

Rethink Revision

Have you ever taken part in a quiz and thought '*I know this*!', but, despite frantically racking your brain, you just couldn't come up with the answer?

It's very frustrating when this happens, but in a fun situation it doesn't really matter. However, in your GCSE exams, it will be essential that you can recall the relevant information quickly when you need to.

Most students think that revision is about making sure you *know* stuff. Of course, this is important, but it is also about becoming confident that you can **retain** that *stuff* over time and **recall** it quickly when needed.

Revision That Really Works

Experts have discovered that there are two techniques that help with all of these things and consistently produce better results in exams compared to other revision techniques.

Applying these techniques to your GCSE revision will ensure you get better results in your exams and will have all the relevant knowledge at your fingertips when you start studying for further qualifications, like AS and A Levels, or begin work.

It really isn't rocket science either – you simply need to:

- **test yourself** on each topic as many times as possible
- **leave a gap** between the test sessions.

It is most effective if you leave a good period of time between the test sessions, e.g. between a week and a month. The idea is that just as you start to forget the information, you force yourself to recall it again, keeping it fresh in your mind.

Three Essential Revision Tips

1. **Use Your Time Wisely**

   - Allow yourself plenty of time.
   - Try to start revising six months before your exams – it's more effective and less stressful.
   - Your revision time is precious so use it wisely – using the techniques described on this page will ensure you revise effectively and efficiently and get the best results.
   - Don't waste time re-reading the same information over and over again – it's time-consuming and not effective!

2. **Make a Plan**

   - Identify all the topics you need to revise (this All-in-One Revision & Practice book will help you).
   - Plan at least five sessions for each topic.
   - One hour should be ample time to test yourself on the key ideas for a topic.
   - Spread out the practice sessions for each topic – the optimum time to leave between each session is about one month but, if this isn't possible, just make the gaps as big as realistically possible.

3. **Test Yourself**

   - Methods for testing yourself include: quizzes, practice questions, flashcards, past papers, explaining a topic to someone else, etc.
   - This All-in-One Revision & Practice book provides seven practice opportunities per topic.
   - Don't worry if you get an answer wrong – provided you check what the correct answer is, you are more likely to get the same or similar questions right in future!

Visit our website to download your free flashcards, for more information about the benefits of these revision techniques, and for further guidance on how to plan ahead and make them work for you.

www.collins.co.uk/collinsGCSErevision

Contents

GCSE Sociology Workbook

Families

Different Family Forms

1 Which term is commonly used by sociologists to describe families in which one or both partners have a child or children from a previous relationship living with them?
Shade **one** box only. [1]

A Extended ◯

B Symmetrical ◯

C Empty nest ◯

D Reconstituted ◯

2 Describe **one** example of global diversity in families. [3]

....

....

....

....

....

....

....

....

Families

The Functions of Families

3 Discuss how far sociologists agree that the nuclear family is an essential part of British society today.

[12]

Continue your answer on a separate piece of paper.

Families

The Marxist Perspective on Families

4 Identify and explain **one** advantage of using group interviews to investigate married people's attitudes towards marriage and family life.　　[4]

Feminist and Other Critical Views of Families

5 Describe **one** example of inequality in power relationships between family members.　　[3]

Families

Conjugal Role Relationships

6 Identify and explain **one** advantage of using secondary sources to investigate family life in Britain today. [4]

....

....

....

....

....

....

....

....

....

7 Describe the instrumental role in nuclear families. [3]

....

....

....

....

....

....

....

Families

Changing Relationships Within Families

8 Identify and explain **one** disadvantage of using a social survey to investigate the quality of parenting. [4]

_____

_____

_____

_____

_____

_____

_____

_____

_____

_____

_____

Changing Family and Household Structures

9 Describe **one** example of a household in Britain today. [3]

_____

_____

_____

_____

_____

_____

_____

_____

Families

10 Which term is used by sociologists to describe a marriage in which a wife has two or more husbands at the same time? Shade **one** box only. [1]

A Polygamy ⬜   B Polyandry ⬜

C Polygyny ⬜   D Monogamy ⬜

11 Identify **one** possible consequence of divorce for the former partners and explain how you would investigate this consequence using unstructured interviews. [4]

_____

_____

_____

_____

_____

_____

_____

_____

_____

_____

12 Which term is used by sociologists to describe the process by which religion loses significance in society? Shade **one** box only. [1]

A Idealisation ⬜   B Alienation ⬜

C Privatisation ⬜   D Secularisation ⬜

Education

The Role of Education from a Functionalist Perspective

1 Identify **one** function of the education system and explain how you would investigate this function using observation. [4]

The Marxist Approach to Education

2 Describe the correspondence principle in education as outlined by Bowles and Gintis. [3]

Education

3 Discuss how far sociologists agree that the main role of the education system is to produce a workforce for capitalism.

[12]

_____

_____

_____

_____

_____

_____

_____

_____

_____

_____

_____

_____

_____

_____

_____

_____

_____

_____

Continue your answer on a separate piece of paper.

Education

Different Types of School

4 Describe **one** example of a type of secondary school in Britain today. [3]

_____

_____

_____

_____

_____

_____

_____

_____

_____

5 Which term is used by sociologists to describe a type of school that is designed to cater for students of all abilities? Shade **one** box only. [1]

A Comprehensive school ◯   **B** Grammar school ◯

C State school ◯   **D** Public school ◯

6 Describe the tripartite system of education. [3]

_____

_____

_____

_____

_____

_____

_____

Education

Social Class and Educational Achievement

7 Describe **one** home-based factor that could influence students' performance at school. [3]

....

....

....

....

....

....

....

....

The Impact of School Processes on Working-Class Students' Achievements

8 Identify and explain **one** advantage of using a longitudinal study to investigate the effects of banding in schools. [4]

....

....

....

....

....

....

....

....

....

....

Education

Ethnicity and Educational Achievement

9 Which term is commonly used by sociologists to describe a curriculum that is biased towards white, European culture? Shade **one** box only. [1]

A Gendered curriculum ◯

B Biased curriculum ◯

C Ethnocentric curriculum ◯

D Informal curriculum ◯

Gender and Educational Achievement

10 Describe the crisis in masculinity that may be experienced by some males. [3]

_____

_____

_____

_____

_____

_____

_____

Education

11 Which term is used by sociologists to describe the study of people in everyday settings? Shade **one** box only. [1]

A Ethnography ◯

B Cross-cultural study ◯

C Cohort study ◯

D One-shot survey ◯

12 Identify **one** ethical issue that you would need to consider when investigating sub-cultures in a school and explain how you would deal with this issue in your investigation. [4]

Crime and Deviance

1. Identify **one** agency of informal social control and explain how you would investigate this agency using unstructured interviews. [4]

2. Describe **one** example of an agency of formal social control. [3]

Crime and Deviance

Functionalist and Interactionist Perspectives on Crime and Deviance

3 Identify and explain **one** advantage of using a longitudinal study to investigate deviant careers. [4]

....

....

....

....

....

....

....

....

....

....

4 What term is used by sociologists to describe the breakdown of norms in society?
Shade **one** box only. [1]

A Alienation	⭕	**B** Moral panic	⭕
C Anomie	⭕	**D** Deviancy amplification	⭕

Marxist and Feminist Explanations of Crime and Deviance

5 Describe **one** way in which some females may be controlled within the home. [3]

....

....

....

....

....

....

Continue your answer on a separate piece of paper.

Crime and Deviance

Statistical Data on the Extent of Crime

6 Describe the dark figure of crime. [3]

Factors Affecting Criminal and Deviant Behaviour

7 Identify **one** ethical issue that you would need to consider when investigating a deviant sub-culture and explain how you would deal with this issue in your investigation. [4]

Crime and Deviance

Other Factors Affecting Criminal and Deviant Behaviour

8 Describe the class deal that may be experienced by some women. [3]

_____

_____

_____

_____

_____

_____

_____

_____

_____

9 What term is used by sociologists to describe the more lenient treatment of female offenders within the criminal justice system? Shade **one** box only. [1]

A Chivalry thesis ◯

B Double deviancy thesis ◯

C Institutional sexism ◯

D Gender stereotyping ◯

Crime and Deviance

10 Discuss how far sociologists agree that social classes in Britain today have different experiences of the criminal justice system.

[12]

_____

_____

_____

_____

_____

_____

_____

_____

_____

_____

_____

_____

_____

_____

_____

_____

_____

_____

Continue your answer on a separate piece of paper.

The Media and Public Debates over Crime

11 What term is used by sociologists to describe a group that is defined as a threat to society's values?
Shade **one** box only.

[1]

A Folk devil ⬜ **B** Gatekeeper ⬜

C Deviant ⬜ **D** Delinquent ⬜

Social Stratification

An Introduction to Social Stratification

1 What term is commonly used by sociologists to describe the uneven distribution of resources (such as income or power) or opportunities related to, for instance, education and health? Shade **one** box only. [1]

A Social class ○

B Social stratification ○

C Social inequality ○

D Social status ○

Different Views of Social Class

2 Which term is commonly used by sociologists to describe how people see themselves in social class terms? Shade **one** box only. [1]

A Objective class ○

B Subjective class ○

C Class alignment ○

D False class consciousness ○

Factors Affecting Life Chances

3 Describe the glass ceiling in the workplace. [3]

Social Stratification

4 Describe **one** way in which governments have tried to address racial discrimination in the labour market.   [3]

_____

_____

_____

_____

_____

_____

_____

5 Identify and describe **one** agency of gender socialisation.   [3]

_____

_____

_____

_____

_____

_____

_____

_____

Social Stratification

Studies of Affluent Workers

6 Identify **one** type of social mobility and explain how you would investigate this type using questionnaires. [4]

....

....

....

....

....

....

....

....

....

....

....

7 Which term is used by sociologists to describe a process in which affluent working-class families are becoming middle class in their norms and values? Shade **one** box only. [1]

A Proletarianisation ⬜   B Embourgeoisement ⬜

C Alienation ⬜   D Class dealignment ⬜

8 Which term is used by sociologists to describe a family whose lifestyle and social relationships focus on the home and immediate family? Shade **one** box only. [1]

A Modified extended family ⬜   B Symmetrical family ⬜

C Patriarchal family ⬜   D Privatised nuclear family ⬜

Social Stratification

Wealth, Income and Poverty

9 Identify and explain **one** disadvantage of using official statistics to investigate poverty in the UK. [4]

_____

_____

_____

_____

_____

_____

_____

_____

_____

_____

_____

_____

10 Which term is used by sociologists to describe the state of poverty in which people see themselves as living in poverty? Shade **one** box only. [1]

A Subjective poverty ⬚   B Objective poverty ⬚

C Culture of poverty ⬚   D Welfare dependency ⬚

11 Which term is used by sociologists to describe the experience of being shut out from participation in everyday activities and customs that most people take for granted? Shade **one** box only. [1]

A Environmental poverty ⬚   B Relative deprivation ⬚

C Social exclusion ⬚   D Poverty trap ⬚

Social Stratification

Different Explanations of Poverty

12 Discuss how far sociologists agree that rising divorce rates are the most important reason for child poverty in the UK. [12]

Continue your answer on a separate piece of paper.

Social Stratification

Power and Authority

13 Identify and explain **one** patriarchal structure highlighted by the sociologist Sylvia Walby. [4]

Power and the State

14 Describe **one** example of an institution of the state in the UK. [3]

Collins

GCSE Sociology
Paper 1 The Sociology of Families and Education

Time allowed: 1 hour 45 minutes

The maximum mark for this paper is 100.

Instructions

- Use black ink or black ball-point pen.
- Answer **all** questions.
- You must answer the questions in the spaces provided. Do **not** write outside the box around each page or on blank pages.
- Do all rough work in this book.

Information

- The marks for questions are shown in brackets.
- Questions should be answered in continuous prose. You will be assessed on your ability to:
  - use good English
  - organise information clearly
  - use specialist vocabulary where appropriate.

Name: ....

Section A: Families
Answer **all** questions in this section.

---

0 1 Which term is commonly used by sociologists to describe the shame or disgrace attached to particular behaviour? Shade **one** box only.

A Social exclusion ◯

B Social convention ◯

C Social stigma ◯

D Double standards ◯ **[1 mark]**

0 2 Which term is used to describe the criminal offence of marrying when already married to someone else? Shade **one** box only.

A Bigamy ◯

B Serial monogamy ◯

C Polygamy ◯

D Empty shell marriage ◯ **[1 mark]**

0 3 Describe an empty nest family. **[3 marks]**

....

....

....

....

....

....

0 4 Identify and describe **one** example of a dependent family member.   **[3 marks]**

Item A

Data from the Office for National Statistics (ONS) shows that, in 1973, there were 8.4 divorces per 1000 married men and 8.4 per 1000 married women in England and Wales. In general, the divorce rate increased over the next 20 years and, in 1993, the figures stood at 14.3 for men and 14.1 for women.

In 2013, however, there were just 9.8 divorces per 1000 married men and 9.8 per 1000 married women. These rates are similar to the divorce rates in the mid-1970s.

0 5 From **Item A**, examine **one** strength of research using official statistics on divorce. **[2 marks]**

0 6 Identify and explain **one** factor that may have led to an increase in the divorce rate
between 1973 and 1993, as referred to in **Item A**.   [4 marks]

_____

_____

_____

_____

_____

_____

_____

_____

_____

0 7 Identify and explain **one** advantage of using a focus group to investigate arranged
marriage in Britain.   [4 marks]

_____

_____

_____

_____

_____

_____

_____

_____

_____

_____

_____

_____

Item B

In her article on conventional families, Ann Oakley (1982) drew on evidence from research carried out by other sociologists. She argues that conventional nuclear family life is no longer the norm in statistical terms. Yet the idea of the conventional family is still a powerful one in society. People expect conventional family life to bring them happiness.

However, Oakley argues that there are strains beneath the surface. This is seen, for example, in the health problems and depression experienced by family members.

0 8 From **Item B**, identify and describe the research method used by Ann Oakley, including what you know of her perspective on the family. **[4 marks]**

_____

_____

_____

_____

_____

_____

_____

0 9 Identify **one** type of family diversity and explain how you would investigate this type of diversity using unstructured interviews. **[4 marks]**

1 0 Discuss how far sociologists agree that the family is the main source of gender inequality in British society today. **[12 marks]**

....

....

....

....

....

....

....

....

....

....

1 1 Discuss how far sociologists agree that the main function of the nuclear family in Britain today is the primary socialisation of children. **[12 marks]**

....

....

....

....

....

....

Practice Exam Paper 1

Turn over for the next question.

Section B: Education
Answer **all** questions in this section.

---

1 2 Which term is used by sociologists to describe research in which the participants are not aware that they are taking part in a study? Shade **one** box only.

A Overt research ◯

B Covert research ◯

C Non-participant observation ◯

D Informed consent ◯ **[1 mark]**

1 3 Which term is used by sociologists to describe the learning that takes place when people develop knowledge and skills by observing what is happening around them in everyday life? Shade **one** box only.

A Official education ◯

B Official curriculum ◯

C Formal education ◯

D Informal education ◯ **[1 mark]**

1 4 Describe the gendered curriculum in education. **[3 marks]**

....

....

....

....

....

....

1 5 Describe **one** example of a system of stratification based on achieved status.　　　**[3 marks]**

Item C

In 2016, the Sutton Trust published a research report on young people receiving private tuition in England and Wales. The paper drew on a poll carried out by an opinion poll company for the Sutton Trust. The poll asked young people aged 11–16 years about the experience of receiving private tuition in England and Wales. The sample size was 2555 students.

The paper also drew on data from several other sources including the UK Millennium Cohort Study, which had a sample size of 19 000 children aged 11 years.

The Sutton Trust reported that affluent families were more likely to employ private tutors for their children than less affluent families. Children attending private schools were around twice as likely to have private tuition as children attending state schools. Ethnic minority students and girls were more likely to receive private tuition than white students and boys.

In England and Wales over the last decade, the proportion of young people who have received private tuition rose by seven percentage points, from 18 per cent to 25 per cent.

Some students received private tuition to improve their performance in entrance exams.

1 6 From **Item C**, examine **one** strength of the research. [2 marks]

1 7 Identify and explain **one** possible reason why the proportion of young people who have received private tuition is rising. [4 marks]

1 8 Identify and explain **one** disadvantage of using a snowball sample to investigate truancy among secondary school students. **[4 marks]**

....

....

....

....

....

....

....

....

....

....

Item D

Stephen Ball studied the impact of banding on students' experiences of schooling in a mixed comprehensive school. He undertook an intensive case study of one school, observing lessons, participating in the school's daily life as a supply teacher and teaching some timetabled lessons as a regular teacher. The field work was carried out over a period of more than two years.

Ball took notes during his observation of lessons and wrote these up as transcripts. He also kept diary notes to record his observations.

1 9 From **Item D**, identify and describe the research method used by Ball, including what you know of his perspective on education. **[4 marks]**

2 0 Identify **one** expectation that teachers might have of students in the top band and explain the possible impact of this expectation on students' educational achievements.   **[4 marks]**

2 **1** Discuss how far sociologists agree that students' family backgrounds are the most important factor in explaining differences in their educational achievements.   **[12 marks]**

Turn over for the next question.

2 2 Discuss how far sociologists agree that feminism is the main reason for the improvements in the educational achievements of girls over the last 40 years. **[12 marks]**

End of questions

Collins

GCSE Sociology

Paper 2 The Sociology of Crime and Deviance and Social Stratification

Time allowed: 1 hour 45 minutes
The maximum mark for this paper is 100.

Instructions

- Use black ink or black ball-point pen.
- Answer **all** questions.
- You must answer the questions in the spaces provided. Do **not** write outside the box around each page or on blank pages.
- Do all rough work in this book.

Information

- The marks for questions are shown in brackets.
- Questions should be answered in continuous prose. You will be assessed on your ability to:
  - use good English
  - organise information clearly
  - use specialist vocabulary where appropriate.

Name: ....

Section A: Crime and Deviance
Answer **all** questions in this section.

---

0 1 What term is used by sociologists to describe the deal that offers women emotional and material rewards in return for living with a male breadwinner within a family? Shade **one** box only.

A Class deal   ◯

B Gender deal   ◯

C Double standards   ◯

D Dual-worker family   ◯   **[1 mark]**

0 2 What term is used by sociologists to describe a research method that involves collecting data through in-depth interviews with participants? Shade **one** box only.

A Questionnaire   ◯

B Structured interview   ◯

C Unstructured interview   ◯

D Participant observation   ◯   **[1 mark]**

0 3 Describe **one** example of an issue of public concern in the UK related to crime.   **[3 marks]**

....

....

....

....

....

....

0 4 Describe agenda setting in the media with reference to crime. **[3 marks]**

Item A

Sociologists can help the authorities deal with football hooliganism by studying the people involved and what motivates them. Research suggests that most football hooligans are working-class males aged 18 to 24 years. John Williams, Eric Dunning and Patrick Murphy (1989) worked together on a project in the Department of Sociology at the University of Leicester that explored football hooliganism among English fans at away games in Europe. The fieldwork was based on three covert participant observation studies. John Williams carried out all three studies. This was because he was young enough, street wise enough and interested enough in football to be able to pass as an everyday English football fan. The researchers explored the norms and values of the youths and young men involved in football hooliganism.

0 5 From **Item A**, examine **one** strength of the research. [2 marks]

0 6 Identify and explain **one** factor that may have led young men to engage in football hooliganism, referred to as a concern in **Item A**. [4 marks]

0 7 Identify and explain **one** disadvantage of using a self-report study to investigate white-collar crime.

[4 marks]

Item B

Merton, a North American sociologist, explains crime and deviance in terms of the structure and culture of society rather than focusing on people's genes or personalities.

Merton argues that people's aspirations and goals (what they see as worth striving for) are largely determined by the values of their culture. The problem is that some individuals and groups accept the goal of achieving economic success but lack opportunities to succeed through legitimate (or socially acceptable) means. Some people end up experiencing strain between the goals they have been socialised to strive for and the means of achieving them.

In this situation, where there is a mismatch between goals and means, a condition of anomie (or normlessness) develops. In other words, the norms that regulate behaviour break down and people turn to whatever means work for them to achieve material success. When anomie develops anything goes, and high rates of crime and delinquency are likely.

Merton identifies five possible ways that individuals respond to success goals in society. Some of these responses (such as innovation, ritualism and retreatism) involve crime and deviance.

0 8 From **Item B,** identify and describe **one** response to success goals in society that Merton highlighted, including what you know of his perspective on crime and deviance. **[4 marks]**

_____

_____

_____

_____

_____

_____

_____

_____

0 9 Identify **one** ethical issue you would need to consider when investigating the victims of crime and explain how you would deal with this issue in your investigation. **[4 marks]**

_____

_____

_____

_____

_____

1 0 Discuss how far sociologists agree that inadequate socialisation at home is the main reason for delinquency among young people. **[12 marks]**

1 1 Discuss how far sociologists agree that police-recorded crime statistics do not accurately reflect the true level of female criminality. **[12 marks]**

Practice Exam Paper 2

Section B: Social Stratification
Answer **all** questions in this section.

---

1 2 What term is commonly used by sociologists to describe social positions that are fixed at birth? Shade **one** box only.

A   Ascribed status ⃝

B   Achieved status ⃝

C   Monarchy ⃝

D   Social status ⃝   [1 mark]

1 3 What term is used by sociologists to refer to government by the people? Shade **one** box only.

A   Dictatorship ⃝

B   Democracy ⃝

C   Pluralism ⃝

D   Rational legal authority ⃝   [1 mark]

1 4 Identify and describe **one** example of a social construct.   [3 marks]

....

....

....

....

....

| 1 | 5 | Describe the process of embourgeoisement that may be experienced by some affluent workers. **[3 marks]**

....

....

....

....

....

....

....

....

....

....

Item C

Irene Zempi and Neil Chakraborti (2014) studied the experiences of Muslim women who wear the niqab (a face-covering or veil) in public places in Leicester. The research was based on 60 semi-structured interviews with veiled Muslim women. In addition, one of the researchers, Irene Zempi (who describes herself as a white, Orthodox Christian woman) wore a veil in public places such as on public transport, in shopping centres and on the streets of Leicester for four weeks. This allowed her to understand more fully the women's experiences as victims of Islamophobia (hostility towards Muslims and Islam) in their daily lives.

For veiled Muslim women, the fear of being attacked and incidents of victimisation can have significant consequences, such as loss of confidence and depression. It can also limit Muslim women's movements, leading to social isolation.

Practice Exam Paper 2

1 6 From **Item C**, examine **one** strength of the research.   **[2 marks]**

1 7 Identify and explain **one** way in which religious hate crime might affect people's life chances as experienced by many of the women referred to in **Item C**.   **[4 marks]**

1 8 Identify and explain **one** disadvantage of using structured interviews to research people's experiences of racism in the UK. **[4 marks]**

....

....

....

....

....

....

....

....

....

....

....

....

Item D

Peter Townsend (1979) investigated how many people were living in poverty in the UK, their characteristics and problems. He used a large-scale questionnaire survey and collected data on 2052 households and 6098 individuals. The national questionnaire survey covered household resources and standards of living.

Townsend calculated that almost 23 per cent of the population were in poverty. He identified particular groups of people who were at risk of poverty. These included elderly people who had worked in unskilled manual jobs, and children in families of young unskilled manual workers or in one-parent families.

1 9 From **Item D**, identify and describe the research method used by Peter Townsend, including what you know of his perspective on poverty. **[4 marks]**

_____

_____

_____

_____

_____

_____

_____

_____

_____

2 0 Identify **one** group that is at risk of poverty in the UK and explain why this particular group is at risk of poverty. **[4 marks]**

Practice Exam Paper 2

2 1 Discuss how far sociologists agree that ethnicity is the most important source of inequality in British society today.

[12 marks]

Turn over for the next question.

2 2 Discuss how far sociologists agree that power is distributed widely in contemporary British society.

[12 marks]

End of questions

There are no questions printed on this page.

Answers

Different Family Forms

1. **D**
2. **Suggested answer:** Kibbutzim in Israel – in a kibbutz settlement, people have a collective way of life rather than living in privatised nuclear families. Originally, children lived together in children's houses and were brought up collectively, but today they are likely to live with their parents until they are teenagers. Meals are taken in communal dining halls. [Maximum 3 marks]

The Functions of Families

3. **Possible content: up to 4 marks for AO1; up to 4 marks for AO2; up to 4 marks for AO3.**
   - Define the term nuclear family and indicate that the traditional nuclear family is declining in statistical terms.
   - Draw on the functionalist perspective (e.g. Murdock and Parsons) to argue that the family performs essential functions for individuals and society.
   - Criticise the functionalist approach.
   - Draw on Marxist perspectives to argue that the nuclear family has an economic function which makes it essential to capitalism.
   - Criticise the Marxist approach.
   - Draw on feminist perspectives to argue that the nuclear family is essential to the workings of patriarchy.
   - Criticise the feminist approach.
   - Argue that attitudes to the nuclear family have changed and people now have more choice about how they organise their personal lives (e.g. living alone or remaining single).
   - Reach a balanced conclusion that addresses 'how far'.

The Marxist Perspective on Families

4. **Example answer:** Practical advantages in saving time and money. [1] In a group interview, the researcher would interview several married people together. They could gather a lot more data about attitudes to marriage and family life from a bigger sample of married people than with individual interviews, which are relatively time-consuming and expensive. [3] **Other possible advantages:** Accessing a range of views; interviewees may feel more comfortable/empowered in a group setting; the group interview might generate fresh ideas – **1 mark for a relevant advantage and 3 marks for explaining this advantage.**

Feminist and Other Critical Views of Families

5. **Suggested answer:** Domestic violence, which can be seen as a form of power and control in which one family member tries to dominate others. This is usually – but not always – perpetrated by men and can be seen as a form of male power and control over women. [Maximum 3 marks]

Conjugal Role Relationships

6. **Example answer:** High-quality secondary sources on family life are readily available, which cuts down on the time and costs compared to gathering primary data. [1] A sociologist could access high-quality official statistics on family life in Britain today (e.g. marriage and divorce rates) and also draw on qualitative data from existing studies of family life carried out by reputable sociologists to save time and money. [3] **Other possible advantages:** Official statistics on marriage and divorce rates allow trends to be identified; research by other sociologists can provide a starting point for fresh research; secondary sources may be the only source available; can be used in the process of triangulation – **1 mark for a relevant advantage and 3 marks for explaining this advantage.**

7. **Suggested answer:** From a functionalist perspective, Parsons identified the instrumental and expressive roles in the nuclear family. The instrumental role belongs to the male (the husband/father) and involves working in paid employment outside the home, being the breadwinner and supporting the family financially. [Maximum 3 marks]

Changing Relationships Within Families

8. **Example answer:** Respondents have limited opportunity to develop answers. [1] A social survey contains pre-set questions, some of which are closed. The respondents do not get an opportunity to discuss parenting issues in their own terms, talk about their experiences of parenting in depth, raise new topics about the quality of parenting or explain why they ticked one box rather than another. [3] **Other possible disadvantages:** Qualitative data cannot be gathered; the researcher cannot deviate from the schedule of questions; the researcher has limited opportunity to build rapport – **1 mark for a relevant disadvantage and 3 marks for explaining this disadvantage.**

Changing Family and Household Structures

9. **Suggested answer:** A single-person household, i.e. one person who lives alone. This could be, for example, a young adult living in a bedsit, a person who is recently divorced or who never married, an elderly widow or widower living alone in the family home. The number of single-person households in Britain is rising. [Maximum 3 marks]

Marriage and Divorce

10. **B**
11. **Example answer:** One possible consequence is that the former partners may face loss of emotional support if their friendship groups change. [1] I would draw up a list of key points to cover in the unstructured interviews, e.g. friendship networks and social life during the marriage and after the divorce. I would select a small sample of divorced couples and obtain their informed consent. I would interview them and probe their answers about loss of emotional support in a sensitive way. I would then analyse the contents of the interviews, highlighting themes and relationships in the data, e.g. links between age, gender and emotional support after divorce. [3] **Other possible consequences:** Changes to their household setting; reduction in income; conflict over parenting and property – **1 mark for a relevant consequence and 3 marks for explaining how you would investigate this using unstructured interviews.**
12. **D**

The Role of Education from a Functionalist Perspective

1. **Example answer:** One function of the education system is secondary socialisation. [1] I would design an observation schedule that addresses secondary socialisation, focusing on the teaching and learning of norms and values during timetabled lessons. I would obtain informed consent before undertaking non-participant observation of a range of lessons in three different types of school. Next, I would analyse the data looking at similarities and differences in the socialisation of students in different types of school and identifying any patterns in the data related to students' gender, ethnicity or social class. [3] **Other possible functions:** Gender socialisation; economic function; selection; social control – **1 mark for a relevant function and 3 marks for explaining how you would investigate this function using observation.**

The Marxist Approach to Education

2. **Suggested answer:** From a Marxist perspective, Bowles and Gintis identify a connection or a close fit between school and work under capitalism. For example, at school, the hidden curriculum emphasises authority, rules and discipline. This fits with – and prepares students for – rules and discipline within the workplace. Through this correspondence, education creates a passive, obedient workforce to meet the needs of capitalism. **[Maximum 3 marks]**

3. **Possible content: up to 4 marks for AO1; up to 4 marks for AO2; up to 4 marks for AO3.**
   - Define the term capitalism.
   - Discuss conflict versus consensus approaches to the role of education in society.
   - Argue from a Marxist perspective that the main role of education is to produce a workforce for capitalism; discuss the work of Bowles and Gintis, and Willis.
   - Criticise the Marxist approach.
   - Argue from a functionalist perspective that education has several functions (economic; secondary socialisation; social control) and that education meets the needs of society.
   - Criticise the functionalist approach.
   - Argue from a feminist perspective that the main role of education is to reproduce patriarchy and gender inequality.
   - Criticise the feminist approach.
   - Reach a balanced conclusion that addresses 'how far'.

Different Types of School

4. **Suggested answer:** A public school such as Eton or Harrow. Public schools are independent of the state sector and are funded through the fees that parents pay. Many select their intake through an entrance examination. They market themselves on their academic ethos, traditions and varied extra-curricular activities. **[Maximum 3 marks]**

5. **A**

6. **Suggested answer:** Under the tripartite system introduced in 1944, students sit an 11-plus test at the end of primary school. Based on the results, they are allocated to one of three types of secondary school according to their aptitudes and needs. These are grammar, technical and secondary modern schools. Grammar schools have an academic focus. Technical and secondary modern schools have a more practical or vocational focus. **[Maximum 3 marks]**

Social Class and Educational Achievement

7. **Suggested answer:** How much of the right sort of cultural capital the parents have. Many middle-class parents who have been to university know how the education system works. They also know how to work the system (e.g. when applying for school places in outstanding schools) to maximise the chances that their children will perform well in exams and achieve their potential. **[Maximum 3 marks]**

The Impact of School Processes on Working-Class Students' Achievements

8. **Example answer:** To track changes in student behaviour in different bands over time. **[1]** With a longitudinal study, a researcher could carry out repeat interviews with one year group and their teachers in one school over time. They could focus on the Year 7 intake and track this cohort through to Year 11. The researcher could record any changes in students' behaviour and their attitudes to school over time, comparing the effects of banding on students in different bands. **[3] Other possible advantages:** The researcher can identify patterns in the data and connections between different variables over time; being able to follow up issues identified during previous stages; less reliance on people's memories; rapport building over time – **1 mark for a relevant advantage and 3 marks for explaining this advantage.**

9. **C**

Gender and Educational Achievement

10. **Suggested answer:** This refers to the idea that the traditional masculine identity of some men, such as young working-class men, is under threat. Traditionally, working-class masculine identity was linked to being the breadwinner and working in manufacturing and heavy industries such as shipbuilding. Today, many of these jobs have declined, so men are more likely to work in low-paid insecure jobs in the service sector. **[Maximum 3 marks]**

Perspectives on the Counter-School Culture

11. **A**

12. **Example answer:** Informed consent. **[1]** When researching sub-cultures in secondary schools, I must decide whether the younger students (e.g. those aged under 18) can give informed consent themselves. A member of a school sub-culture might want to take part in the study because they like the attention or the idea of appearing in a book but they might not appreciate any possible disadvantages, so I would deal with this by also asking the parents/carers to consent (or otherwise) on their children's behalf. **[3] Other possible issues:** Confidentiality; anonymity; avoiding harm to participants – **1 mark for a relevant issue and 3 marks for explaining this issue.**

Pages 169–173 Crime and Deviance

An Introduction to Crime and Deviance

1. **Example answer:** The family. **[1]** I would list the areas or points about informal social control in families that I wanted to cover in the interviews. I would identify a sample of middle-class and working-class families whose members would be willing to take part in the interviews about social control and get their informed consent. I would carry out the interviews. Once I had the interview transcripts, I would analyse the contents looking for themes, and similarities and differences between middle-class and working-class families in how social control operates. **[3] Other possible agencies:** Education; religion; peer groups – **1 mark for a relevant agency and 3 marks for explaining how you would investigate this agency using unstructured interviews.**

2. **Suggested answer:** Her Majesty's Prison Service. People who are found guilty of committing more serious crimes could get a prison sentence. The purpose of prison is to punish convicted offenders, rehabilitate them and deter them (and other people) from committing crimes in the future. **[Maximum 3 marks]**

Functionalist and Interactionist Perspectives on Crime and Deviance

3. **Example answer:** Explore the development of deviant careers over time. **[1]** A longitudinal study can investigate an issue over time. A deviant career involves several stages and takes time to develop. By using a longitudinal study, the researcher could identify a group of people who have been publicly labelled as deviant and track their lives over time to investigate why some of them develop deviant careers while others don't. **[3] Other possible advantages:** Building up rapport over time; obtaining a more detailed account of the process of developing a deviant career; participants' memories of events may be fresher – **1 mark for a relevant advantage and 3 marks for explaining this advantage.**

4. **C**

Marxist and Feminist Explanations of Crime and Deviance

5. **Suggested answer:** Women may be controlled at home through marriage, domestic life and motherhood. Many women who are mothers and wives/partners will have fewer opportunities and less time to commit crime than men if most of their time is taken up with domestic work, childcare, controlling children and emotion work. **[Maximum 3 marks]**

Statistical Data on the Extent of Crime

6. **Suggested answer:** The dark figure of crime refers to unrecorded crime – crime that does not appear in the police-recorded crime statistics produced by the state. The dark figure includes crimes without witnesses and unreported

crime. White-collar crime, for example, is more likely to be unrecorded than street crime. Some estimates suggest that official statistics include only a small proportion of all crimes committed. [Maximum 3 marks]

Factors Affecting Criminal and Deviant Behaviour

7. **Example answer:** As a researcher, I have a duty to safeguard the interests of all research participants (even if they belong to a deviant sub-culture) and to make sure they come to no harm as a result of the research. [1] If I observe the members of the sub-culture engaging in deviant acts or committing crimes, I must decide how to write these up in any publications. I would write them up in a way that safeguards the participants' identities; otherwise the members of the deviant subculture could be identified and penalised for taking part in the research. [3] Other possible issues: Informed consent; confidentiality – 1 mark for a relevant issue and 3 marks for explaining how you would deal with this issue.

Other Factors Affecting Criminal and Deviant Behaviour

8. **Suggested answer:** The feminist sociologist Pat Carlen argues that working-class women are expected to make the class deal (as well as the gender deal). The class deal offers them material rewards such as being able to buy consumer goods if they work in paid employment for wages. However, if the rewards are not available or not worthwhile, the deal breaks down. [Maximum 3 marks]

9. A

10. **Possible content: up to 4 marks for AO1; up to 4 marks for AO2; up to 4 marks for AO3.**
    - Define the terms social class and criminal justice system (CJS).
    - Argue from a Marxist perspective that different social classes have different experiences of the CJS. Criminal law operates in the interests of privileged groups and, for example, benefit fraud is seen as more serious than tax evasion. The agencies of social control target street crime rather than white-collar or corporate crime. They also target working-class people.
    - Criticise the Marxist approach.
    - Argue from an interactionist perspective that different social classes experience labelling within the CJS differently. The police, for example, may label and target working-class people. Becker argues that some groups have the power to make the rules and enforce them. Power is related to social class, gender and ethnicity.
    - Argue from a feminist perspective that gender is more significant than class in influencing people's experience of the CJS. Men and women have different experiences of the CJS, e.g. through the chivalry effect and double deviance.
    - Argue that ethnicity is more significant than class, e.g. the police have been linked to institutional racism.
    - Reach a balanced conclusion that addresses 'how far'.

The Media and Public Debates over Crime

11. A

Pages 174–179 Social Stratification

An Introduction to Social Stratification

1. C

Different Views of Social Class

2. B

Factors Affecting Life Chances

3. **Suggested answer:** The glass ceiling refers to an invisible barrier in the workplace that stops women getting promoted to the top posts in industry, the legal profession, education, etc. This explains why men and women who work in the same profession are often found at different levels of the hierarchy, with men dominating the higher positions. [Maximum 3 marks]

4. **Suggested answer:** Introducing legislation to tackle racial discrimination at work by making it illegal and providing a means for people to challenge and stop it. In the 1970s, the Race Relations Act made racial discrimination illegal in employment. The Equality Act 2010 aims to promote a more equal society and outlaws discrimination based on race in employment. [Maximum 3 marks]

5. **Suggested answer:** The family is an agency of gender socialisation. Parents and other relatives distinguish between babies from birth according to their gender by dressing them in pink or blue and describing them in different ways. The term canalisation refers to the way parents channel their children's interests towards gender-appropriate activities, toys and games. [Maximum 3 marks]

Studies of Affluent Workers

6. **Example answer:** Inter-generational mobility. [1] I'd start by designing a questionnaire that asks respondents about their own social class background and career history, as well as that of their parents. Next, I'd identify a representative or typical sample of adults who would give informed consent and fill in the questionnaire. Once the questionnaires were completed, I'd analyse the data by looking for patterns of mobility according to social class, age, gender and ethnicity, and for any connections between these factors. [3] **Another possible type:** Intra-generational mobility – 1 mark for the relevant type and 3 marks for explaining how you would investigate this type using questionnaires.

7. B

8. D

Wealth, Income and Poverty

9. **Example answer:** No control over the measurement of poverty. [1] As a secondary source, official statistics are put together by the state for administrative purposes rather than by sociologists for research purposes. The definition and measurement of poverty used by the state may be different from those a sociologist would prefer to use. As a result, the statistics might misrepresent and underestimate the true level of poverty in UK society. [3] **Other possible disadvantages:** lack of qualitative, in-depth data; the statistics tell us nothing about what poverty means to people – 1 mark for a relevant disadvantage and 3 marks for explaining this disadvantage.

10. A

11. C

Different Explanations of Poverty

12. **Possible content: up to 4 marks for AO1; up to 4 marks for AO2; up to 4 marks for AO3.**
    - Define the terms divorce and poverty.
    - Outline which children are most vulnerable to poverty.
    - Argue from a feminist perspective that lone mothers have a high risk and long duration of poverty. Possible reasons include the gender pay gap.
    - Examine other possible reasons for child poverty such as the cycle of deprivation.
    - Argue from a Marxist perspective that child poverty results from class-based inequalities in capitalism rather than from rising divorce rates.
    - Argue that child poverty is linked to unemployment, welfare state inadequacies and globalisation rather than to rising divorce rates.
    - Reach a balanced conclusion that addresses 'how far'.

Power and Authority

13. **Example answer:** Paid employment. [1] Walby argues that the labour market segregates occupations by gender (e.g. fire fighters and nursery nurses) and women are in the worst jobs. Women typically earn less than men and are excluded from the better types of paid work. For many women, wages are so low that paid work is not really worthwhile in financial terms. [3] **Other possible structures:** The household; culture; sexuality; male violence; the state – 1 mark for a relevant structure and 3 marks for explaining this structure.

Power and the State

14. **Suggested answer:** The police force. The police are an agency of formal social control in UK society and their role is to maintain order, enforce the law, investigate crime and apprehend people who break the criminal law. [Maximum 3 marks]

Section A: Families

01 C

02 A

03 **Suggested answer:** An empty nest family consists of a couple whose adult child or children have moved out of the family home (e.g. to set up their own home with a partner or to take up employment in another area). The couple now live together in a two-person family household. They are usually aged in their 40s, 50s or older, and may be retired. [Maximum 3 marks]

04 **Suggested answer:** One example of a dependent family member is a child aged 0–15 or aged 16–18 in full-time education. They live with their parent or parents, e.g. in a lone-parent or nuclear family. They have not yet completed their full-time compulsory education, are too young to be financially independent of their parents, and are likely to depend on their parents for emotional support. [Maximum 3 marks]

05 **Example answer:** One strength is that official statistics on divorce provide quantitative data that is collected on a national level from a reputable source following official standards and guidelines. [1] As a result, the statistics are likely to provide an accurate measure of divorce. [1] **Other possible strengths:** Reliability; generalisation is possible; can identify trends over time; an accessible and cheap source of data for sociologists studying divorce – **1 mark for a relevant strength and 1 mark for showing why this is a strength.**

06 **Example answer:** Higher expectations of marriage. [1] During that time, people began to expect more from their marriage. This was partly due to the way the media represented romance in films and pop songs. So people were no longer prepared to stay in a relationship that did not fulfil their hopes or needs. They were more likely to get divorced and possibly to look for fulfilment in a second marriage. [3] **Other possible factors:** Legal changes; less stigma attached to divorce; impact of secularisation; the changing social and economic status of women – **1 mark for a relevant factor and 3 marks for explaining this factor.**

07 **Example answer:** Explores how participants interact and respond to each other's views on arranged marriage. [1] The interviewer can explore how the interviewees respond to each other when they discuss their experiences of, and views on, arranged marriage in Britain. For example, do they support or dismiss alternative views, or does anyone change their mind about arranged marriage? This would provide an extra dimension over and above what would be possible in one-to-one interviews. [3] **Other possible advantages:** the ability to explore the theme of arranged marriage in depth; gather qualitative data; participants may feel more comfortable/empowered in a group setting; the focus group may generate new ideas about arranged marriage – **1 mark for a relevant advantage and 3 marks for explaining this advantage.**

08 **Suggested answer:** The research is based on secondary sources of information/a literature review. [1] Writing from a feminist perspective, Oakley uses pre-existing sources including the work of other sociologists. She uses the information to provide a critical analysis of the conventional nuclear family, including its financial inequality linked to gender. Oakley contrasts the idea of the conventional nuclear family with the reality and argues that living in conventional families can be stressful. [3] **1 mark for identifying the relevant research method. Up to 3 marks for describing the method and the perspective.**

09 **Example answer:** One type of family diversity is social class diversity. [1] I would begin by noting down the themes or areas I wanted to cover in the interview, such as social class differences in role relationships and child-rearing practices. I would then identify a sample of working-class and middle-class couples who would be willing to give informed consent. I would carry out the unstructured interviews. I would analyse the interview transcripts by coding sections to identify any key themes, similarities and differences in conjugal roles and child-rearing practices between the social classes. [3] **Other possible types of diversity:** Cultural, life-course, cohort and organisational diversity – **1 mark for a relevant type of diversity and 3 marks for explaining how you would investigate this type using unstructured interviews.**

10 **Possible content: up to 4 marks for AO1; up to 4 marks for AO2; up to 4 marks for AO3.**
   - Define the term gender inequality.
   - Describe gender socialisation including canalisation within families as a source of inequality.
   - Draw on feminist perspectives to argue that the nuclear family is the main source of gender inequality in society today. Discuss Delphy and Leonard's views on hierarchy and economic exploitation within families, and their views on patriarchy in families.
   - Discuss inequality in power (e.g. decision making and domestic violence) in families.
   - Draw on Sylvia Walby's feminist approach to argue that the family is one of several patriarchal structures in society, including paid employment, culture and sexuality.
   - Criticise the feminist approach.
   - Draw on Marxist approaches to argue that gender inequality within families is linked to the workings of capitalism rather than patriarchy. Men as well as women are oppressed under capitalism.
   - Draw on the functionalist approach to argue that the nuclear family is functional rather than unequal. It meets the needs of individuals and society.
   - Reach a balanced conclusion that addresses 'how far'.

11 **Possible content: up to 4 marks for AO1; up to 4 marks for AO2; up to 4 marks for AO3.**
   - Define the terms function, nuclear family and primary socialisation.
   - Draw on the functionalist perspective to argue that the main function of the nuclear family is the primary socialisation of children.
   - Draw on Parsons' functionalist account of the two key functions: primary socialisation and stabilisation of adult personality.
   - Describe other important functions of the nuclear family such as reproduction.
   - Criticise the functionalist approach. Point out, for example, that some critics argue that many children are inadequately socialised within the family and/or that it is more relevant today to consider 'diverse families' rather than 'the nuclear family'.
   - Draw on feminist approaches to argue that the main role of the nuclear family today is to reproduce patriarchy.
   - Criticise the feminist approach.
   - Draw on the Marxist approach to argue that the main function of the nuclear family is to reproduce capitalism.
   - Criticise the Marxist approach.
   - Reach a balanced conclusion that addresses 'how far'.

Section B: Education

12 B

13 D

14 **Suggested answer:** In a gendered curriculum, some subjects (including high status subjects such as maths and science) are associated with masculinity and others (such as languages and humanities) are associated with femininity. These ideas can influence (and limit) students' subject choices at school, their higher education course choices and future careers. [Maximum 3 marks]

15 **Suggested answer:** The social class system of stratification is based on achieved status. It is meritocratic and status is based on an individual's talents and abilities rather than their birth. Equal opportunities exist and working-class students can achieve qualifications through their own abilities, experience upward social mobility and get a middle-class job. **[Maximum 3 marks]**

16 **Example answer:** One strength is the size of the different samples. One sample had 2555 students and the other had 19 000 children. **[1]** The research covers a lot of students so the sample is more likely to be representative (compared to a smaller sample) or typical of the wider population of students. **[1] Other possible strengths:** Drawing on data from several sources; an opinion poll can be replicated to check the reliability of findings – **1 mark for a relevant strength and 1 mark for showing why this is a strength.**

17 **Example answer:** Impact of the economic recession on job opportunities. **[1]** Following the global recession and the limited job opportunities for young people, affluent parents might believe that there is more pressure on their children to achieve top grades in their GCSE and A Level exams in order to get into a prestigious university and enter a professional career. Affluent parents can afford to pay for private tuition as a way of investing in their children's futures during a recession. **[3] Other possible reasons:** More testing of students; more pressure to perform well in SATs; more pressure to pass the 11-plus exam/school entrance exam/ university entrance exam; increased competition within education – **1 mark for a relevant reason and 3 marks for explaining this reason.**

18 **Example answer:** The researcher is not in full control of the sample selection process. **[1]** Rather than select a random sample from school registers, snowball sampling means that the researcher has to rely on the willingness of secondary school students to identify their peers who truant. A student who truants might not want to identify other truants in case s/he gets them into trouble, or in case their parents/ teachers find out. This means that things like luck or chance play a part in the sample selection process. **[3] Other possible disadvantages:** Unlikely to generate a large sample; the researcher may not gather sufficient data; the sample will not be random/representative/typical of the wider population; the researcher cannot generalise – **1 mark for a relevant disadvantage and 3 marks for explaining this disadvantage.**

19 **Suggested answer:** Ball used participant observation as his research method. **[1]** He studied banding and mixed-ability teaching at Beachside Comprehensive School to explain the underperformance of working-class students. This was an ethnographic case study that focused on people in an everyday setting. Ball's perspective is partly interactionist because he explores the interactions between teachers and students but he also pays attention to the wider structure of the school. He is now a leading sociologist who studies social inequality within education. **[3] 1 mark for identifying the relevant research method. Up to 3 marks for describing this method and Ball's perspective on education.**

20 **Example answer:** One expectation is that students in the top band will achieve the highest grades at GCSE. **[1]** If teachers expect students in the top band to do well academically, this can act as a positive label. It could encourage these students to work harder than they otherwise would and strive for the top GCSE grades. The teacher could also push these students to improve their performance. In this way, high expectations could lead to a self-fulfilling prophecy in that the original prediction comes true. **[3] Other possible expectations:** Expecting students in the top band to complete a lot of homework; expecting students to prioritise school work; expecting students to stay on to study A Levels; expecting students to progress to university – **1 mark for a relevant expectation and 3 marks for explaining the impact of this expectation.**

21 **Possible content: up to 4 marks for AO1; up to 4 marks for AO2; up to 4 marks for AO3.**
   - Outline the differences in educational achievements between students based on their social class, ethnicity and gender.
   - Argue that students' family backgrounds are the most important factor. Examine the influence of factors linked to family backgrounds on educational achievement. Such factors include material deprivation, cultural deprivation, parental values and expectations, parents' educational backgrounds and cultural capital.
   - Examine the influence of peer groups within the neighbourhood on educational achievement.
   - Argue that school-based factors and processes are more important than family background. Examine the influence of factors such as teacher expectations, labelling and the self-fulfilling prophecy on different students' educational achievements.
   - Examine the influence of school-based factors such as the school ethos, student cultures and anti-school sub-cultures on the achievement of different students.
   - Argue that schools are meritocratic and that educational achievement is linked to individual effort.
   - Examine factors such as school-based resources, the quality of teaching, the gendered curriculum and the ethnocentric curriculum on achievement.
   - Argue that educational policy is most important. Examine factors linked to policy such as the impact of marketisation on different students and schools; the impact of equal opportunities policies and anti-discrimination legislation.
   - Reach a balanced conclusion that addresses 'how far'.

22 **Possible content: up to 4 marks for AO1; up to 4 marks for AO2; up to 4 marks for AO3.**
   - Outline the improvements in girls' educational achievements, such as their improved performance in public examinations; increased likelihood of progressing to university. However, subject choices within FE and HE are still gendered.
   - Argue that these improvements are mainly due to feminism. Examine the impact of feminism on girls' attitudes to education, careers, gender roles and financial independence.
   - Argue that the improvements are due to more girl-friendly schooling/the feminisation of education and changing assessment patterns such as coursework assessment. However, the curriculum is still gendered.
   - Argue that the improvements are due to teachers' higher expectations of female students, labelling and the self-fulfilling prophecy.
   - Argue that the improvements are mainly due to legislation/changing government policies such as the Sex Discrimination Act (1975), the Equality Act (2010) and the introduction of the National Curriculum.
   - Argue that, despite the improvements, some feminists still see the education system as patriarchal.
   - Reach a balanced conclusion that addresses 'how far'.

Pages 200–219 Practice Exam Paper 2

Section A: Crime and Deviance

01 B
02 C
03 **Suggested answer:** One example is sentencing policy and the sentencing of convicted offenders. People are not always clear about how sentencing works. For example, when offenders are released from prison early, people do not necessarily understand why this happens. The media sometimes fuel this public concern by reporting on early release prisoners who go on to commit further crimes. **[Maximum 3 marks]**

04 Suggested answer: Agenda setting refers to the media's power to set the focus of public debate about crime. The media do not tell people what to think but they do tell people what to think about. They do this by focusing on some groups and issues (such as illegal immigrants and street crime) and excluding others (such as corporate crime). Possible effects of this are that some groups become scapegoats, or the media create moral panics. **[Maximum 3 marks]**

05 Example answer: One strength is that John Williams was young, street wise and interested in football so he could successfully play the role of a football fan and undertake all three covert participant observation studies. **[1]** This allowed him to gather rich and detailed qualitative data about incidents of football hooliganism as they unfolded. **[1] Other possible strengths:** The research was covert so there is no observer effect; by doing participant observation, the researcher captures events first hand rather than relying on what people tell them in interviews; the researcher is able to see the world through the eyes of the hooligans – **1 mark for a relevant strength and 1 mark for showing why this is a strength.**

06 Example answer: The young men's socialisation within the home/neighbourhood. **[1]** The young men may have been socialised to value being 'macho' and to express their masculinity by drinking alcohol, vandalism and fighting with other men who they see as outsiders. So football is used as a context for fighting, violence and expressing masculinity. **[3] Other possible factors:** Status frustration among working-class males; peer group pressure; sub-cultural values and norms; fighting as a source of excitement and meaning; deviancy amplification in the media – **1 mark for a relevant factor and 3 marks for explaining this factor.**

07 Example answer: One disadvantage is the low validity of the responses. **[1]** Professional people in high status jobs might be unwilling to admit that they have been involved in undetected white-collar crime such as tax evasion or fiddling their expenses at work. Even though the researcher promises them anonymity and confidentiality, they may think it is not worth admitting any involvement because, if the truth came out, the consequences could be quite severe. In other words, they have nothing to gain and too much to lose by being honest in a self-report study. **[3] Other possible disadvantages:** Lack of opportunity to build rapport; lack of detailed, in-depth qualitative data; limited opportunity to explore the reasons behind white-collar crimes – **1 mark for a relevant disadvantage and 3 marks for explaining this disadvantage.**

08 Suggested answer: One response to success goals is innovation. **[1]** In this case, individuals accept the culturally defined goals (such as getting rich) but they lack opportunities to succeed through legal means. So these people innovate by turning to crimes such as theft or fraud to get rich. Merton examined the causes of crime and deviance from a functionalist perspective. He applied the concept of anomie (normlessness) to crime and deviance. He argued that if people experience a mismatch between the goals and the means, then the norms break down and people turn to any means available to achieve economic success. **[3] 1 mark for identifying a relevant response to success goals. Up to 3 marks for describing this response and Merton's perspective on crime and deviance.**

09 Example answer: One issue is the potential to cause distress to the research participants. Some victims of crime may feel upset or vulnerable when discussing their experiences. **[1]** These feelings may become more intense when taking part in research based, for example, on unstructured interviews. I would deal with this by explaining in advance what the questions are likely to involve, emphasising that participation is voluntary and that the participant has the right to withdraw from the research at any point without having to give a reason. **[3] Other possible issues:** Informed consent; anonymity; confidentiality; potential consequences for research participants such as being victimised for taking part – **1 mark for a relevant issue and 3 marks for explaining this issue.**

10 Possible content: up to 4 marks for AO1; up to 4 marks for AO2; up to 4 marks for AO3.
- Define the terms delinquency and socialisation.
- Draw on functionalist approaches to describe the importance of primary socialisation in families as a means of teaching norms and values. Argue that inadequate socialisation in families is the main reason for delinquency.
- Argue that other agencies of socialisation (e.g. religions and schools) are also failing to socialise children effectively and contributing to delinquency.
- Draw on Albert Cohen's sub-cultural theory to argue that delinquency among working-class boys is linked to status frustration at school rather than to socialisation at home.
- Argue that some sociologists do not focus on home factors. Interactionism, for example, focuses on the interaction between young people who commit delinquent acts and those who react to these acts.
- Draw on Marxist approaches to argue that certain groups (such as young people, particularly inner-city and working-class youth) are more likely to be targeted by the police and to be seen as delinquent.
- Reach a balanced conclusion that addresses 'how far'.

11 Possible content: up to 4 marks for AO1; up to 4 marks for AO2; up to 4 marks for AO3.
- Define female criminality and describe police-recorded crime statistics.
- Outline the gendered patterns of crime shown in police-recorded crime statistics: females commit fewer crimes, less serious crimes and are less likely to reoffend than men.
- Taking the statistics at face value, women may commit fewer crimes because they have less opportunity to offend. For example, their domestic role and triple shift mean they have less time to offend. Females are also more closely controlled than men.
- Taking the statistics at face value, it may be that gender socialisation processes encourage females to be passive and to avoid conflict and crime.
- Argue that the statistics underestimate the true level of female criminality because the police act with chivalry towards female offenders and treat them more leniently than males. So the police are less likely to arrest and detain female offenders and to record female crime. On the other hand, the double deviance theory suggests that women who commit crime (particularly women who do not conform to feminine stereotypes) are treated more harshly than men.
- Argue that police-recorded crime statistics are socially constructed and underestimate the level of crime committed by females, particularly middle-class females.
- Reach a balanced conclusion that addresses 'how far'.

Section B: Social Stratification

12 A

13 B

14 Suggested answer: One example of a social construct is gender. While sex (being male or female) is a biological construct, gender (masculinity and femininity) varies between cultures and over time. It is created by society through the process of primary socialisation in families. Gender is reinforced through secondary socialisation, e.g. through the gendered curriculum in schools. **[Maximum 3 marks]**

15 Suggested answer: The embourgeoisement thesis argues that affluent working-class families are becoming middle class in their norms and values due to an increase in their income and improvements in their standards of living. They now have privatised lifestyles centred on their home and family. **[Maximum 3 marks]**

16 Example answer: One strength is that the female researcher carried out a form of ethnography by wearing a niqab in public. This allowed her to gain direct experience of Islamophobia and to understand more fully how Muslim women experience this. **[1]** As a result, she could empathise with/build up rapport with the Muslim women and collect more in-depth and detailed accounts during the interviews. **[1] Other possible strengths:** The ethnography was covert so there is no observer effect; the researcher does not have to rely solely on what interviewees tell her in interviews; the ability to gather qualitative data that is likely to be valid – **1 mark for a relevant strength and 1 mark for showing why this is a strength.**

17 **Example answer:** Religious hate crime can affect people's life chances by affecting their health (including their mental health) in a negative way. **[1]** In this case, religious hate crime increased the women's chances of experiencing depression. If they are repeat victims of religious hate crime, this could affect their chances of being healthy or ill as they progress through life. **[3] Other possible ways:** Limiting the women's employment opportunities; limiting their opportunities to pursue higher education; contributing to their social exclusion – **1 mark for a relevant way and 3 marks for explaining this way.**

18 **Example answer:** Lack of flexibility. **[1]** Structured interviews are based on a pre-set schedule of questions and all interviewees answer exactly the same questions about their experiences of racism. If an interviewee raises a point about racism that the researcher had not anticipated, the interviewer cannot follow up this new line of enquiry by asking fresh questions about it. **[3] Other possible disadvantages:** The lack of opportunity to build rapport compared to unstructured interviews; lack of opportunity to gather detailed qualitative data about racism; potential for interview/interviewer bias – **1 mark for a relevant disadvantage and 3 marks for explaining this disadvantage.**

19 **Suggested answer:** The method was a large-scale questionnaire survey that was delivered face-to-face by a big team of interviewers across the UK. **[1]** This landmark survey asked about people's household resources and standards of living. Townsend developed a deprivation index to measure the extent of poverty (or relative deprivation) in the UK. He was a pioneer in the study of poverty because he focused on deprivation and viewed it in relative terms. **[3] 1 mark for identifying the relevant research method. Up to 3 marks for describing this research method and Townsend's perspective on poverty.**

20 **Example answer:** One group is elderly people, particularly older women. **[1]** Older people who rely on the state retirement pension may be at risk of poverty. They have to live on a relatively low income if they do not have an income from a workplace pension or a personal pension that they contributed to during their years at work. Older women are less likely to have built up an occupational pension than older men. **[3] Other possible groups:** Lone-parent families; women; some minority ethnic groups; children – **1 mark for a relevant group and 3 marks for explaining why this group is at risk of poverty.**

21 **Possible content: up to 4 marks for AO1; up to 4 marks for AO2; up to 4 marks for AO3.**
- Define ethnicity and inequality.
- Argue that ethnicity is the most important source of inequality by looking at issues such as racism, average earnings, average household income, unemployment, educational underachievement, poverty and the under-representation of some minority ethnic groups in positions of power in Britain.
- Argue that some minority ethnic groups are better placed than others, e.g. in terms of educational achievement, so it is inappropriate to generalise.
- Draw on Marxist approaches to argue that in capitalist society, social class is the most important source of inequality. Discuss issues such as working-class educational underachievement and life chances in relation to income, health, housing and social mobility.
- Draw on feminist approaches to argue that gender is the most important source of inequality in patriarchal society. Discuss issues such as gender inequality at work, the glass ceiling, the gender pay gap, the risk of poverty, sexism and female under-representation in positions of power.
- Argue that age and disability are the most important sources of inequality in contemporary British society.
- Argue that all forms of inequality (including those based on sexuality) are significant and they should be seen as interrelated or linked rather than as separate aspects.
- Reach a balanced conclusion that addresses 'how far'.

22 **Possible content: up to 4 marks for AO1; up to 4 marks for AO2; up to 4 marks for AO3.**
- Define the term power.
- Draw on the pluralist approach to argue that political power is distributed widely (e.g. through pressure groups, trade unions and direct action groups) and no single group dominates. The role of the state is to regulate the different interests in society.
- Draw on the conflict approach to argue that power is concentrated in the hands of a minority whose members come from privileged backgrounds. Unelected groups such as chief executives of multinational corporations exercise power by influencing government policy.
- Draw on Marxist approaches to argue that power in capitalist society is linked to social class relationships. Members of the bourgeoisie hold power based on their ownership of the means of production. The state protects the interests of members of the bourgeoisie.
- Draw on feminist approaches to argue that power is concentrated in male hands in patriarchal society. Discuss Sylvia Walby's work on patriarchy in British society.
- Reach a balanced conclusion that addresses 'how far'.

Notes

Notes

Notes

Notes

Collins GCSE Revision

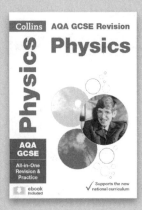

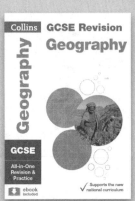

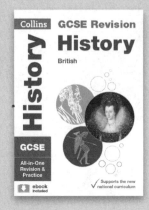

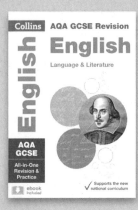

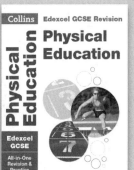

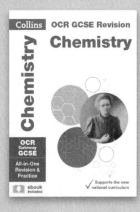

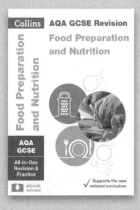

Visit the website to view the complete range and place an order:

www.collins.co.uk/collinsGCSErevision

ACKNOWLEDGEMENTS

The author and publisher are grateful to the copyright holders for permission to use quoted materials and ima

Cover, p.1, p.153 © Rawpixel.com/Shutterstock.co
© zimmytws/Shutterstock.com,
© tadamichi/Shutterstock.com
All other images © Shutterstock.com

Every effort has been made to trace copyright hold and obtain their permission for the use of copyrigh material. The author and publisher will gladly recei information enabling them to rectify any error or omission in subsequent editions. All facts are corre at time of going to press.

Published by Collins

An imprint of HarperCollins*Publishers* Ltd

1 London Bridge Street,
London, SE1 9GF

© HarperCollins*Publishers* Limited

9780008227456

First published 2017

10 9 8 7 6 5 4 3 2

British Library Cataloguing in Publication Data.

A CIP record of this book is available from the Britis Library.

Authored by: Pauline Wilson
Commissioning Editors: Katherine Wilkinson and Charlotte Christensen
Editor: Charlotte Christensen
Project Manager: Tracey Cowell
Cover Design: Sarah Duxbury and Paul Oates
Inside Concept Design: Sarah Duxbury and Paul Oa
Text Design and Layout: Jouve India Private Limited
Production: Natalia Rebow
Printed in the UK, by Martins The Printers
Printed and bound by: Grafica Veneta in Italy

6 EASY WAYS TO ORDER

1. Available from www.collins.co.uk
2. Fax your order to 01484 665736
3. Phone us on 0844 576 8126
4. Email us at education@harpercollins.co.
5. Post your order to: Collins Education,
   FREEPOST RTKB-SGZT-ZYJL,
   Honley HD9 6QZ
6. Or visit your local bookshop.